Love-Making

From the Inside Out

*Transform Conflicts, Complaints and Criticism
into a loving relationship*

Dr. Bill Cloke

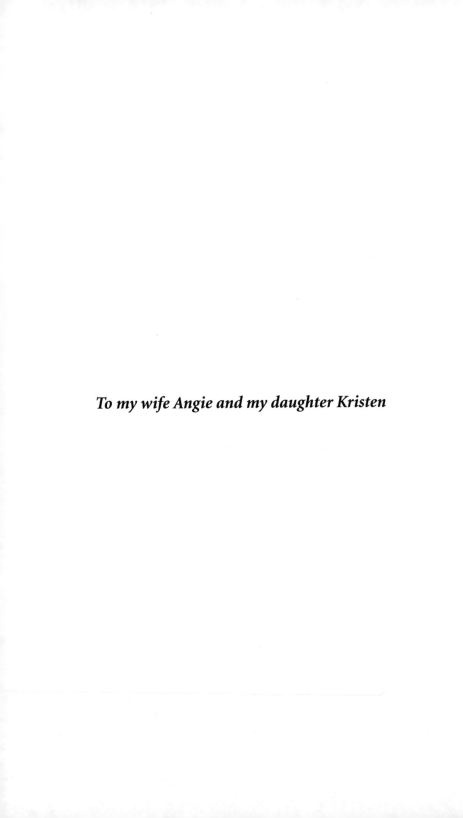

To my wife Angie and my daughter Kristen

Contents

Acknowledgements

I thank my mother Shirley Cloke for being an indomitable spirit of positive energy and a loving, supportive and eternally loyal mom. She remains my very dearest friend.

To my beautiful daughter Kristen who grew up with me and with her loving honesty and patience encouraged me to become a therapist.

To my brilliant wife Angie who inspired me to write this book, put up with me through all the years of writing it and loved me for all the right reasons. Her vulnerability and loyalty have been the spirit that has given me the strength to finish this project.

To my professors and mentors Drs. Ted Carpenter, Council Taylor, Avendis Panajian, Jack Delchamps, Russell Hunter, Susan Johnson, Daniel Wile, John Gottman, Bill Ofman, Beverly Frank, and to Vida Van Brunt, John Huston, Martin Beaudet. To Dr. Esther Benton whose intelligence, compassion and love have been a model for what it means to be authentic and caring.

To my accomplished brother Ken Cloke and his wife Joan Goldsmith for setting the bar that inspired me to do my best work, and for lending their support to this project.

A special thanks to Rick Richman for lending his support and ideas to this book.

To my remarkable patients who have over the years taught me so much about perseverance, tolerance and love. They have given me my most valuable insights which have enabled me to become a better therapist. The vignettes in this book are composites of people I have worked with and the names and specifics have been changed to protect their privacy.

Thank you all.

Introduction

Oh the comfort, the inexpressible comfort of feeling safe with a person, having neither to weigh thoughts nor measure words, but pouring them all right out, just as they are, chaff and grain together; certain that a faithful hand will take and sift them, keep what is worth keeping, and then with the breath of kindness blow the rest away.

Dinah Maria Mulock Craik, 1826

Is happily-ever-after actually attainable? Is it possible to continue to love and be loved by someone for a lifetime? Love-Making: *From the Inside Out* is about the very intricate process of how love is made. This book will unveil the mysterious alchemy of how love and romance are actually created on a far grander scale than just when eyes meet across a crowded room. Love is an active process that can be fashioned into something that is at once durable and yet a thing of beauty. To create love, we need to distinguish how our underlying and baffling personal issues impact our ability to make an enduring love. To engender love we need to know how conflict and personal pain can be a resource for deeper intimacy. Love is an unrivaled life experience because it flows from an open heart and a curious spirit. It's a flame that can burn for a lifetime if tended to with kindness and compassion. Relationships are a living thing, requiring both honesty and innovation to be exciting and spontaneous. With the ongoing processes of insight, tolerance and inspiration, we can build a safe and secure relationship for long term love-making.

Couples Who Made It:

- Understand how negative interactions can break their precious connection to each other.
- Have made a distinction between how they felt as children

and who they are as adults.

- Are attuned to each other in a way that enables them to be truly empathic.

- Have grasped how their communications cause deeper feelings to emerge, and handle them in a way that leads to a more intimate connection.

- Understand that the core components for long-term love-making are compassion and empathy: compassion because it enables the development of precious insights into the inner world of their partner, and empathy because it's the best process for resolving conflicts.

- Recognize that the goal of love-making is to create love rather than expecting love.

The critical components for the longevity of a loving relationship lie in how we love and knowing who we are. True and abiding love is the result of being caring and kind. It requires self-reflection about what we want and who we want to be. It means that we have done some personal work to understand how experience has affected us. It necessitates that we have some knowledge about what impedes or helps us maintain an intimate connection. If we appreciate how these sometimes covert processes affect our ability to love, we will be able to work through inevitable disappointment more successfully. Clearly expressing what we need, want, and value, and our willingness to see our partner do the same, will lead to greater relational health. These basic concepts are the life-blood of every healthy relationship.

Because lasting love is *made*, it can be both liberating and inspiring, and extend to our families and communities. Loving couples impact everyone; they offer us optimism and lead us toward deeper insights about ourselves. But most of all, loving relationships infuse us with hope for a better future and a more humane society. This book is dedicated to all those who yearn to build a loving relationship that will not only stand the test of time, but flourish.

The Journey Begins

It was a hot summer day in Santa Monica back in 1983, when Jake and Brenna walked into my office for their weekly therapy appointment. I was testing my new video recorder and wanted to try it out on them. I got their permission and started it rolling.

They were an attractive couple in their mid-forties and were married just two years when their conflicts began to escalate. Jake seemed bewildered when he arrived, so I asked him what was bothering him. They had quarreled earlier that day, and he couldn't grasp why Brenna was so upset. She had accused him of raging at her about money, and she did not feel good about the way he had spoken to her. Jake denied raging and insisted that he was only trying to make his point. He was making one excuse after another.

About a half-hour into their discussion with me about finances, Brenna blurted out, "Jake, you are just so cheap!" Jake, who had forgotten about the camera, bolted upright, screaming, "How dare you say that when all you do is spend, spend, and spend." He launched into a rage that left Brenna in tears.

Money issues were their hot button. They had been down this road before, always with the same outcome. Brenna melted into the sofa and wept while Jake raged. This was their dance—they were a train wreck. As they were leaving, I handed Jake the videotape to review before our next session.

The next day Jake phoned up horrified. He sputtered, "Who was that on the tape?" It was shocking to realize that he did not recognize himself as he was in the video. How could this be? I was filled with curiosity about how he could be so blind to himself. Although Jake's behavior was extreme, I had observed the same behavior in other patients who couldn't see how their personal issues were being expressed toward others.

From such incidents, I began searching for answers as to what had caused the contradictory quality of Jake's encounter with himself and his wife. How could someone experience a powerful emotion like rage and not be aware of it? Why is it that some relationships withstand rage, infidelity, or loneliness while others break apart? What are the internal mechanisms that produce love, and compassion? How are love and intimacy created, and how are they destroyed? How does our inner world affect and create our outer world in relationships with others?

What became apparent during my decades-long search into the nature of passionate attachments were the multifaceted elements that were present in all love relationships. Over the years since Jake and Brenna arrived, I have endeavored to understand what makes love last.

Four Major Themes Emerged

- No matter how much love and passion there is in the beginning of a relationship, for love to last a lifetime it must be actively made, created by a collaborative process whereby couples work together to make and maintain an emotional connection.
- The key to love-making is our ability to use self-knowledge and teamwork to resolve conflicts. If these things are done properly, the resolution process will lead to a deeper intimacy.
- The challenge for loving couples is to become the kind of people who are worthy of being loved, and to develop an atmosphere within and between each other where it can thrive.
- And finally, the goal of love-making is to form a loving relationship that is both safe and secure, a touchstone for comfort and harmony.

An important facet of long-term relationships is the commitment couples make toward maintaining their connection with each other. The deeper our commitment to love-making the greater the possibility it will remain vital and alive. Creating an enduring emotional connection *does* take energy and focus, but the miracle is that love can last and become more satisfying over time. Lasting love is made from the concerted effort of two people crafting their own unique relationship from the sweat and toil of daily life and from all the difficulties, hardships, and conflicts that arise in sharing a life together.

Having a firm grasp on how to reprocess lost connections is an essential relationship skill for keeping love alive. Creating a high-energy emotional bond with discernable methods for withstanding the inevitable storms confronting us all is the goal of love-making. *Critical to understanding how intimacy is created and maintained is to accept that it is a function of and is intertwined with our inner life.* The outcome of working through our personal issues is that we become more compassionate, understanding, respectful, and empathic toward others because it is happening inside. The more we're able to be inwardly accepting, the more we're able to be outwardly tolerant. Understanding how our life experience affects our sense of who we are is an important part of building an authentic emotional life with our mate.

Part of what it means to love another person is to accept that we are intimately bound to each other, not only for our basic need to be loved and connected, but also because we have made a commitment to persevere. Recognizing that an emotional connection with others is essential for our psychological health is the essential pathway toward a more fulfilling life. However, commitment does not mean that we have license to act badly. Our dedication to each other must be based on our willingness to listen attentively and behave respectfully.

People frequently ask, "Why are relationships so resistant to change? We read books, we go to seminars, yet our problems persist." Unraveling the secrets of how love is made requires a bigger perspective than what can be found in seminars, books, or television self-help programs. Distinguishing who we are from who we are with is half the battle. By constructing a psychological map of the territories below the surface and beneath the armor that we construct to protect us, we will be less likely to dump our personal pain onto those we love.

Another fundamental quality of love-making is the ability to form strong attachments and from this create a safe and secure relationship. Safety and security are the cornerstones of all lasting love relationships. They allow us to open up about feelings, fears, and our secrets. In this way, self-knowledge, trust, and safety create the basic conditions for intimacy, enabling couples to comfort each other in times of stress and continue loving each other.

How This Book Is Organized

- **Chapter One** centers on a discussion about how to create love from everyday life.

- **Chapter Two** begins an odyssey through the straits and narrows of relationship life by defining and describing intimacy and how to keep it.

- **Chapter Three** considers conflict and the role it plays in creating intimacy.

- **Chapter Four** shows us how myths and fantasy contribute to our relationship and how they can provide valuable insights into ourselves and others.
- **Chapter Five** explores the role of sexuality in our relationship life.

- **Chapter Six** opens with a characterization of what makes us happy and conversely what makes us unhappy and how to look at them both constructively. It concludes with a look at how moods and fear affect the way we love or the way we defend against loving.

- **Chapter Seven** is an exposition on the value of creative complaining and how to unlock the doors of negativity without breaking our precious connection with our partner.

- **Chapter Eight** is a discussion of why monogamy matters and the effect of extramarital affairs on intimacy and trust.

- **Chapter Nine** defines shame, anger and rage, and explains how they impact us and our ability to love. It's a detailed presentation of how shame affects us, and a crucial chapter for all those who suffer from the issues of anger and shame.

• **Chapter Ten** discusses how couples can beat the odds and come out on top.

• **Chapter Eleven** is about what it takes to live happily ever after, summarizing the important elements of love-making.

And So....

Simply put, we get *out* of relationships what we put *into* them. Relationship happiness is a direct result of deliberate actions that elevate and intensify feelings or shut them down, depending on how we behave. We need to be willing to express the hard truths such as how afraid or hurt or unlovable we feel, or that we don't trust love can last. The goal is to discover the truth within ourselves and communicate it, not to injure, but to engage our partner in a process that leads to greater closeness and love.

If we are willing to risk opening our hearts and minds, we will find ourselves in a universe that we never knew existed. Binding our heart with another and finding its strength uncovers what is so precious about life. Love is what gives life its color and fills us with its meaning. It's what keeps us sane and feeds our soul. As we build a loving relationship we allow ourselves to love someone for who they are, not in spite of it, and we can create a vision of who *we* are from behind our lover's eyes.

1

How Love is Made

What cannot be said will get wept.
Charles McGrath

Why we fall in love is mysterious and complex but continuing to love that same person over a lifetime is the ultimate personal challenge—not only to maintain a loving relationship, but to improve upon it. For love to last a lifetime, vital elements need to fit together, from an ongoing sex life, to a satisfying lifestyle, to developing the ability to connect deeply through compassionate honesty, to having worked out a way to get through the basics of everyday life. The way a relationship begins is often a far cry from what it's like after many years of being together. The day-to-day pace of life, daily rhythms, moods, health issues, and levels of flexibility or rigidity are but a few of the factors that make up a marriage or relationship. If our partner asks for help and we don't give it, or if we feel entitled to scream obscenities when we're angry, or if we don't get what we want when we want it, or if we are unwilling to listen to the needs of our partner, there will be serious consequences. To maintain a healthy relationship it's imperative that we know how to listen with considerate interest and with an open mind. To ensure that the love we began with is still there ten or twenty years in the future requires some necessary steps.

The Steps

- Lasting love requires that each person be fully committed and willing to do the work that produces an emotional connection.
- Each person must feel safe and secure, so that they can express themselves without judgment or criticism.

- There must be active kindness, compassion, empathy, and understanding present in daily interactions.
- We need to be aware of what our personal issues are so we know what to do when they appear.

We may feel we know what's right and wrong in an intimate relationship, but it's often more difficult than we think. There are in all of us hidden processes just below the surface that can jump out at us at a moment's notice.

What is Love?

We begin our exploration into love relationships by first trying to define what love is. There are many shapes and styles to loving someone, from loving friendship, to being infatuated by love at first sight, to romantic love that is created after infatuation fades, to consummate loving that is formed out of an intimate process over many years of being together. True love is the complete package of connecting with our head, heart, body and soul. It is the coming together of our sense of attraction with our ability to uniquely and mutually create a harmony of connection in the same way.

Pioneer psychologist Harry Stack Sullivan wrote that love is the condition where the needs and feelings of the other are as or more important than our own. Author and existentialist Jean Paul Sartre wrote of love as a wish or call for the other to come out. Freud is well-known for describing the two most important conditions in life as love and work. Milan Kundera describes love as interrogation. These notions of love all have a common theme: an intense feeling that pulls one's thoughts and desires toward the loved one.

J. Richard Udry in *The Social Context of Marriage* cites a survey of various college students' ideas about love.

Their Responses:

- Love represents a magnetic attraction between two persons.

- Love is a feeling of high emotional affiliation that sends a person's ego to dizzying heights.
- Love is the result of a mature union of two compatible personalities.
- Love is helping the other person whenever they need it, being a companion. It's about having common goals, dreams, and ambitions.
- Love is doing things together and liking it.
- Love is giving—time, understanding, yourself.
- Love is giving trust.
- Love is a give-and-take relationship—mostly give.
- Love is based on the security of feeling wanted and the certainty that we can rely on that person. Security creates a sense that the world is safe.
- Love to me is faithfulness to my mate and caring for our children.

People have made war, spent fortunes, and even died, all in the name of love. Diane Ackerman writes in *A Natural History of Love*:

So it is with love that values, customs, and protocols may vary from ancient days to the present, but not the majesty of love. People are unique in the way they walk, dress, and gesture, yet we are able to look at the two people—one wearing a business suit, the other a sarong—and recognize that both of them are clothed. Love also has many fashions, some bizarre and (to our taste) shocking, others more familiar, but all are part of a phantasmagoria we know. In the Serengeti of the heart, time and nation are irrelevant. On that plain all fires are the same fire.

Romance 101

Romance is the stuff of grand gestures, selfless acts, and consuming feelings of *'til death do us part*. We yearn for romance and to be filled with the contentment that the thought of love conjures up. It's an active process, and continuing to be romantic in the humdrum of daily life is a challenge. For most men a romantic partner will be tied up with sexual attraction, loyalty, an accomplished career, and/or the potential to be the mother of his children. Generally in our society, most women want to be cherished, someone they can count on and will be a good provider, a caring person. Many people believe that marriage is about letting loose with whatever comes to mind. But romantic relationships require much more.

Where Romance May be Hiding

While working with a couple who were angrily criticizing each other, I could see that they were locked in a negative cycle. The wife berated her husband for never making plans to go out, never bringing her flowers or helping her around the house so they could spend time together on the weekends. Her husband sat quietly shaking his head, feeling hurt by the criticism.

I said to her, "I think you are actually saying something quite romantic." She looked at me quizzically. I explained that everything she was pointing out in a negative way was also about her sense of what she wanted from a loving relationship. I repeated back to her in positive language that she was asking to spend more time with her husband and that she wished he would do things like bring her flowers to show his love for her so that she would feel cherished. She wanted love and support, and even though she was expressing it by criticizing him, her romantic message was tucked away beneath it. She didn't feel safe enough to express her deepest romantic feelings. They both acknowledged that this was true. She was so afraid her husband didn't share her feelings that she couldn't risk being positive and vulnerable. When he felt criticized, he became defensive and then withdrew.

The rest of the session went differently. As he understood the feelings that lay beneath her criticism, he was much more willing to respond lovingly. We went on to discuss all the activities that created more love between them and agreed that they needed to continue to talk about what loving meant to each other and how best to express it. When she was able to grasp the idea that taking the risk of expressing her vulnerability could help her get what she wanted, she was more willing to go there.

What Promotes Romance Over Time?

One answer is to create reality-based romantic talk. Something like, "When you talk to me about what you want and things that you are thinking about doing, especially when it includes me, it makes me love you more." The response might be, "I want you to know what I'm thinking and how important you are to every decision I make."

During a discussion with a couple who were making wedding plans, the bride-to-be expressed frustration with her wedding planner. Their typical way of reacting to a problem was to re-enact both of their family processes, which involved getting angry and blaming each other in a defensive tirade. After the initial distance they would recover only to later have a similar experience with the same result. This time in therapy, after some work and mutual realizations, they had a different experience. He decided to take over the responsibility of dealing with the wedding planner for his fiancée. He had been afraid to take control for fear of doing it wrong and being criticized. He took a risk. At our next session she turned to him with tears in her eyes and said that this was the first time in her life that she felt truly supported and loved. Her family would have criticized her. She would have criticized him. Instead, she said it made her love him more. We went on to discuss how his decision to take charge helped her feel cared about. He seized the opportunity to be supportive and helpful, and at that critical moment he actively created more love. In this short vignette one of the central concepts of love-making is illustrated. It is a conscious choice emanating out of a deep understanding of our own and our partner's needs and feelings. Often, the best results are achieved by acting counter-intuitively, which in this case would have been to act differently than what he had always done and what was done to him. The secret here was that he took the opportunity to create more love by doing something that he knew she needed. She had never experienced someone supporting her in this way. They went on to have a fabulous wedding.

If we have experienced pain around needing support, we might have difficulty accepting it from our mate. Then our natural state would be to defend against fearful, vulnerable feelings and automatically respond defensively. Doing those things that we know are meaningful to our mate is a key to love-making. It's not necessarily smooth or seamless to go against our internal grain, but when our goal is to create more love, we can focus our attention on what we need to do to make it so. If we can stop for a moment and think about what our partner needs and try to respond while still being aware of our own feelings, we will more often be rewarded with a positive response.

What Complicates Love

It's not so much that it's not easy to fall in love, for when it happens it feels natural and enjoyable; it's staying in love that's difficult. So how can we preserve love without projecting these struggles onto our partner? What causes difficulties in our ability to continue loving our mate are both the internal processes that govern our behavior, and the defenses that spill onto our relationship.

Clearly, the more we know about these processes and defenses, the better we will be at controlling their impact on our loved ones. This is what it means to create love from the inside out.

Love is sensitive to all interactions between people. Love-making compels us to pay attention to and draw distinctions between who we are and who our partner is. The more pain we're in, the more we will lay it on our partner. The interaction both internally and externally between wants, needs, desires and personal pain, form the ecosystem within and between loved ones. Sustaining love requires that we not only articulate our internal life to our mate, but that we also risk exposing what we believe are negative aspects of ourselves.

Our worst fear is that exposing our pain, expressing needs and allowing our feelings to be known will cause criticism, humiliation or abandonment. The opposite is usually true. Not expressing needs, wants, and feelings will more likely cause rejection or at the very least alienation. Communicating our internal dialogue is the best chance we have for continuing a loving relationship. Bringing feelings, complaints, hurts, and misunderstandings to the surface and perhaps working them through is the activity of love-making. When there are many unresolved issues between people, it creates distance and interrupts their ability to feel loving toward each other. The trouble is, most people are simply using what they know, and many times this knowledge fails them. More understanding is required. We must not only comprehend what happens inside when we feel criticized, rejected, or judged, but be able to factor that knowledge into our conversation with our partner, especially during conflicts. Clearing away what obstructs our ability to love is an essential part of what it means to love over time.

Love-Making Dialogue

> *Him:* "When you withdraw, it scares me. My parents withdrew from me when I didn't behave the way they wanted, and my girlfriends rejected me because I didn't behave the way they wanted, so when I get angry or upset with you I'm afraid to show it because I'm afraid that you'll throw me away. So I throw you away first."

> *Her:* "I will never throw you away because you get mad at me, but I will get upset if you don't tell me what's bothering you. It always comes out anyway. We have to tell each other how we feel without tearing away our love for each other. When I say something that is insensitive and you shut down, and then I get more angry and critical, we are just repeating our old patterns. How can we make this different?"

This dialogue contains all the elements of effective communication between partners. The more we're able to create these kinds of conversations, the better we will be at love-making. This kind of discussion allows couples to reprocess their interactive style. The key elements here are support, understanding, and a willingness to reflect about their own behavior. Using self-knowledge and feelings to resolve issues together creates a compassionate and loving outcome. For love to prosper we need to make and maintain loving connections with our partner. The stronger these connections are the more lasting our love will be. Love and romance are nurtured by small things as well as large gestures. A patient recently explained to me that he had taken his wife on many wonderful vacations but listening to her we found that it was condescending attitude, controlling behavior and constant anger that made her feel unloved.

Here are some basic concepts to work on as a couple in your every day world.

The Foundation for Love

• *Friendship:* Treat your mate the same way you would treat your best friend. We sometimes forget how vital being a good friend is to fostering love.

• *Consideration:* To be considerate about the things that are important to your mate is essential for harmony. Helping out, remembering important events and agreements, and doing things your partner wants are small gestures that can have a large effect over time.

• *Fairness:* It creates balance within the relationship. Sharing household chores, vacations, spending, friends and responsibilities toward relatives creates more harmony and positive feelings.

• *Tolerance:* Our ability to tolerate our partner's foibles and flaws is important for lasting peace. Tolerance for differences in feelings, ways of doing things, parenting styles, and the other opposing views that all couples possess is a key component to love-making.

• *Acceptance:* Acceptance of each other is an important element in establishing safety. Acceptance is the bedrock of a secure relationship. Security is the foundation for love. Being unconditionally accepted for reprehensible behavior is not part of acceptance. Acceptance is feeling like we are not too much trouble or too odd to be loved.

• *Responsibility:* Being able to own our part of a problem is required for conflict resolution. One of the main reasons for divorce is the inability of one person or the other to accept responsibility for difficulties in the relationship.

• *Support:* When you support your partner, you are sending a message that you believe in him or her and you are on their side. Support is about helping to fulfill dreams and aspirations and providing care when your partner is sick or defeated.

• *Willingness to listen:* When you listen, you connect. Listening is the key to understanding, which opens the door to deeper connections.

• *Respect:* Showing a mutuality of respect for the feelings, needs, and ideas of your partner is fundamental to building a sense of safety. Feeling safe allows feelings to emerge from hiding. Being respectful and considerate are daily activities that create the atmosphere for love to grow.

• *Emotional availability:* The ability to make your feelings known not only helps resolve conflicts but expresses what we want and for that matter, what we don't want. Making your feelings available to your partner allows them to respond in a positive way. This creates closeness.

• *Kindness:* What more needs to be said? It's always better to be kind than entitled, right or superior. Kindness works in most situations.

- *Tenderness:* This is one of the most important processes for love-making. This is how you soothe hurt, fear and sadness. Tenderness is the emotional salve that causes your mate to feel seen and cared about.

- *Compassion:* Showing compassion is the active part of listening. It shows that you are truly there and are hearing what is being said.

- *Self-acceptance:* The reason why some couples don't have to work so hard is that many small things roll off their backs and they can keep going with a positive attitude. Self-acceptance means they do not have to be perfect to feel okay about who they are.

- *The ability to bear ambivalence:* This is the act of staying even when everything in you wants to split. Being angry, turned off and ready to run yet staying, listening and fighting hard during tough times is an essential skill for long-term relationships.

- *Making time for sex or affection or both:* When couples actively create space and time for sex and affection, they will more often be able to achieve contentment. Physical and emotional contentment is what supports monogamy. One of my patients asked me "What about being spontaneous?" I said, "Make time to be spontaneous."

- *Sense of humor:* Many disagreements, tensions, and angry feelings can be neutralized with humor. Couples who can laugh together, stay together.

Just as there are methods and means for creating love there are just as many defensive processes that can destroy it. Here are some of the main love killers.

Road Blocks to Love-Making

These behaviors illustrate common defenses:

- *Globalization:* "Everybody does that."
- *Blame Shifting:* "And you do the same thing but worse."
- *The Victim:* "I'm so good to you, and you treat me so badly."
- *Gaslighting:* "I was just kidding; can't you take a joke?"
- *Entitlement:* "You are the one who made me angry; You deserve it."
- *Denial:* "I'm not angry."
- *Displacement:* "Just because you had a bad day at work, don't take it out on me."
- *Guilt:* "I work my ass off to give you everything and you can't even make me some tea."
- *Shame/Blame:* "You are a human slug; you never do anything."
- *Stonewalling:* "This is the way I am; take it or leave it."
- *Projection:* "You think I'm stupid, don't you?"
- *Devaluation:* "You really could lose some of that extra weight."

Who Do We Appreciate?

What is it that creates love, and what destroys it? While expressing appreciation itself will not make or break a relationship, it is a positive step. Appreciation affirms good deeds: "Thank you for cooking such a great dinner. I realize that you went to a lot of trouble, and I really appreciate it." Gratitude is a means of sustaining feelings of happiness and love. The expression of something positive, even in an argument, helps to smooth it out. Love grows in an atmosphere of appreciation. So often couples can't understand why their partner is distant and angry, only to learn that it is caused by them not feeling appreciated. What appears to be a ubiquitous and general truth is that men crave appreciation and women want to be cherished. Love is like a garden, the more we tend it the more beautiful it becomes. Some people feel that expressing appreciation is a sign of weakness. Nothing could be further from the truth. Gratitude is the grease that makes the relationship wheel run smoothly and encourages positive behavior.

As we look at what it takes to sustain a loving relationship, it may appear to be quite daunting. I try to support couples by explaining that if they can learn effective problem solving, it will only be difficult in the beginning. If we can evaluate and understand what caused the negative interactions both from our own assessment, but also from listening to what our partner is telling us, our expectations will in time, meet with reality. It may be many months or even years between conflicts once we know how to create a loving environment that is rich with humor and loving kindness.

The Importance of Being Earnest

The earnest efforts to create shared values are the bulwark of relationship stability. Establishing mutually agreed upon values is like finding level ground. It's like a compass that directs us toward a balanced relationship that's always moving forward. What supports love-making are principles, opinions, feelings, ethics, and morals that represent what is important to both people. Our behavior defines us more than our words.

As I sit with couples who are fighting about an issue that seems so crucial at the time, I will often say, "What's more important, your relationship or being right?" They usually stop because what I am saying rings true. They get lost in their own hurt, in being righteous and trying to win. When establishing our values, we set the rules of engagement, like how to show respect and concern during discussions. We must try to include our different points of view to resolve arguments. Staying true to our values during the most difficult times is another key to love-making.

Some Values That Serve Love-Making

- Loving and caring trumps everything else.
- Your relationship comes before being right.
- Listen first, then talk.
- When angry, stop, cool down first, then think about what's bothering you and your partner, and assemble your feelings into a coherent statement that includes your values: "What's important to me is that you respect me."
- No yelling, swearing, or name calling.
- Never hit below the belt.
- Never blame, shame, or criticize.
- Never take what's being said personally; instead, find out what's hurting you or your mate.
- Never assume. When in doubt, check it out.
- Listen to what your mate is telling you about you, and then try to apply it.
- What can you do to make it better?
- Find out what is creating the break in your connection.
- Be true to yourself.
- Be true to your word.

Some Ideas About Writing Our Own Code

What guides us through the ups and downs of relationship life is our moral and ethical code for behavior. We all need to know where we are and what we believe to be true about how we want to live our lives, both personally and professionally. Lawrence Kohlberg, the renowned developmental psychologist, created a paradigm for his hierarchy of moral development. He believed that moral codes are active developmental processes. He defined his hierarchy by explaining that moral development is learned over time and begins in childhood. First, we behave according to what our parents believe is right and wrong, and then we behave in ways that fit with what others believe is right and wrong. Next, we take our cues from what larger society believes is correct in an effort to fit into the cultural world of conventional wisdom. The final or highest level of moral development according to Kohlberg is to have formed our own moral code by internalizing our personal and moral beliefs. To him, true moral development is when the final authority for moral judgment is ourselves. To not be ashamed of ourselves is then our highest moral value.

The motion picture *High Noon* starring Gary Cooper and Grace Kelly tells the story of a small town sheriff who stuck to his moral code in the face of mighty opposition from his wife and the entire town. The townsfolk were more concerned about saving themselves than standing up to a gang of outlaws bent on destruction. The sheriff can be seen as a heroic figure because he decides that his moral belief that standing up to a gang of thugs is more important than the entire town (including his wife) turning against him. He could not have lived with himself if he hadn't fought the injustice.

For couples, the development of their own moral processes and belief systems provides a steadying influence in their relationship. Agreed-upon values are especially helpful for creating security. To develop our moral code we must question, scrutinize, evaluate, and enunciate those values we hold to be important. Developing strong values and moral codes helps our relationship run more smoothly.

Heart and Soul

To truly understand what healthy interactions are all about, we need to consider the complexity of what may be causing conflicts with our mate. An argument about putting the cap back on the toothpaste may contain clues to buried feelings. The toothpaste conflict may actually be related to a sense of feeling invisible, or needing to control, and the cap is the way our feelings are ignited. Feeling helpless or invisible may be at the core of the conflict, but the toothpaste is where the argument is focused. Many couples scratch their heads and wonder how such an innocuous comment could lead to such a big fight. The clue to what is causing the conflict may lie under the toothpaste conflict and into each person's life history and personal issues.

When we find ourselves in a fight that cycles around and around, it's a dead giveaway that something deeper is going on. When an argument seems locked in a negative cycle, always take it down a few levels. Recognizing where we're hurting is a positive precursor to working the conflict through. If we believe that we are essentially stupid and inadequate, how are we going to react to any form of criticism? So often at the heart of a conflict is a completely different set of feelings. Looking, seeing, and understanding what is hurting us and then doing the same thing with our partner is the first step. Next, we need to determine where the negative feelings are coming from. Once we are clear about the origin of the problem, we can make better choices about what we need to say. This new perspective, which is derived from our understanding of ourselves and our partner, can move us toward compromise, reconciliation, and a fresh approach to the conflict. Resolution must include mutual respect, tolerance for differences and a willingness to listen to those differences with an open mind.

After a nasty conflict, it may take a long time for loving feelings to return. It's difficult enough to open up to each other, and it is impossible in an unsafe environment. Taking a step back, considering our feelings, and then talking about what's hurting us or what we need is critical to love-making. When conflicts are handled with care, concern, interest, and empathy, we are actively preserving our connection.

Conflict Happens

When we fall in love, we have only a limited knowledge of our partner; we haven't yet been through difficulties, losses, and stressful situations together. Over the years, the full extent of our personality—good and bad—will become known. The everyday routines and the vagaries of existence bring out all aspects of our personalities and along with them, our personal issues. There are the usual mundane relationship conflicts, time conflicts, energy level conflicts, temperature conflicts, television, music, food, time, and value conflicts that happen in the normal course of living. How we handle daily conflicts relates not only to our partner but to our relationship with ourselves. If we feel that every disagreement is a signal that we are bad or unlovable or that our side of the conflict is the right and only way, then we're adding to the trouble we are already in. If we are flooded with shame, guilt or rage when a conflict arises, we will have great difficulty separating our internal conflict from our relationship conflict. If our family process was to attack or defend, we will mimic that response during relationship struggles because it's what we know. People with unresolved internal conflicts are prone to be defensive whenever there is a sense that they have done something wrong. *Unresolved personal issues will be externalized in relationship conflicts.*

Internal Conflicts That Affect Love-Making

- *Being uncomfortable in one's own skin*: This is when we believe we must hide our true self and ultimately our truth from our partner. This creates distance and ultimately distrust.

- *Negatively comparing ourselves to others*: This is the outcome of feeling less than others, and it makes us defensive and envious. It's painful to feel that someone has something that we don't or will never have. So, we may try to tear them down to feel better. We can do this either passively by being snide or sarcastic, by being passive/aggressive in ways like not showing up or sabotaging a relationship with a friend, or even by direct criticism and put-downs.

- *Self-critical feelings*: These emanate from perfectionism or idealism. Either way, we become critical of our partner.

- *Idealized expectations toward one's self and others*: Having overly romantic ideals creates disappointment and causes a sense of failure within the relationship and disconnection from our partner.

- *Feeling disorganized and confused*: When we are unable to carry our part of the load, we overburden our partner. This causes resentment and loss of respect.

- *Fear of failure or success*: Fear of success is actually the fear of failure turned upside-down. One dysfunctional member of a relationship can make the relationship dysfunctional.

- *Feeling depressed and anxious throughout the day*: This also causes the relationship to be anxious and depressed.

- *Feeling like the "victim"*: This is a subtle form of punishment that causes the other person to be angry and want to pull away or punish in return. This causes resentment and loss of respect.

- *Hopelessness about the future*: This depresses everyone. In fact, it's the hallmark of depression.

- *Perfectionism*: This serves to make the other person feel criticized or inferior.

- *Helplessness*: Feelings of powerlessness and passivity create distance and inertia.

- *Feeling weak and worthless*: Our mind automatically hides these feelings from our awareness and if not known will ultimately disconnect us from our mate.

- *Feeling blocked or frozen:* This keeps the relationship from moving forward and is a sign of depression within the relationship.

Love over time is the combination of understanding who we are based on life experience, and the way we interact with our partner in regard to their feelings and needs. The ability to weave together what we need to do for ourselves and what we need to give and get from our partner will create a more content and satisfying life. What we need to do for ourselves is to create our own self-esteem, advance in our work or career, and take care of our health and our personal stuff. What we need from others is love, affection, comfort, support (when offered freely), sex and companionship. When successfully married couples are asked the secret of their success, invariably they answer "It takes work." It does take work, but we must remember that it is love's work, and we are rewarded with sweet serenity and a sense that love can last.

The Urge to Merge

Phil and Donna were very happy to find each other. They had spent many years alone and both wanted a relationship. As they became more involved, conflicts began to arise. Feeling especially connected during a make-up period, they decided to get married after one of their most dramatic fights. Conflict was all they knew about being intimate.

Phil and Donna found themselves locked in an emotional prison of their own making. Their conflicts grew out of a series of negative and insulting remarks over small misunderstandings. Phil would mentally make a list of complaints about Donna and withdraw into righteous indignation. Finally, he would whip out the list, and they would fight about it for days. Theirs was an attack/attack conflict style that left them in a heap of frustration that would eventually lead to make-up sex.

Susan Johnson defines three different conflict styles in her book, *The Practice of Emotionally Focused Couple Therapy: Creating Connection*. The first and most common conflict style is attack/defend, wherein one person attacks and the other defends, the second style is attack/attack which is almost always fatal to the relationship because of the volatile nature of both people attacking each other, and thirdly and also often fatal, the defend/defend style which creates immense distance between the couple because neither one will make the effort to connect or resolve the conflict.

Donna had custody of her son from a previous marriage, and Phil had co-custody of a daughter with his former wife. In the first year of their marriage, Phil lost his job. As the months stretched on, the tension became unbearable, and they fought bitterly. Being unemployed and living together, Phil could no longer retreat into work or to his separate home. Phil withdrew into a gloomy depression. At the same time, Donna began to rise within her company and loved every minute of it. She had always relied on men to support her. She was financially independent for the first time in her life. Phil felt rejected and openly criticized her in front of the children. During these battles, Phil would punish Donna by withdrawing and refusing to speak to her. When he did open up, he raged at her with all the vitriol he could muster, and she would do the same thing back to him. They were locked in a negative battle.

Phil had come from an authoritarian household. His father was a tough street kid who came up the hard way, fighting all the way up the corporate ladder. He trained Phil to be strong, never cry, and in no way run from a fight. Phil and his father fought throughout his childhood and adolescence. His mother was the classic victim. She frequently lamented to her son about the plight she was in, and complained of being a slave to his father. Phil identified with both of them. From his father he adopted an authoritarian, aggressive personality, and from his mother he learned to be the victim. From the victim position as the aggrieved party, he felt entitled then to punish Donna. Phil had a quiet charm that impressed people, but when he was angry and aggressive, withdrawn and self-pitying, he was impossible to reach.

Donna grew up in a poor family with an alcoholic father and an overburdened mother. Her father was distant and unavailable but would engage her in heated and passionate conflicts concerning daily chores and other things that she would forget to do. Donna learned to fend for herself throughout her childhood, but after adolescence, she enlisted men to take care of her, especially financially. When she was able to find a good job, her newfound freedom made her very happy but also opened up her anger. She was enraged at her critical and tyrannical father and vowed to herself that she would never again be controlled by a man. Her anger at her father and distrust of men caused her to hold in her feelings and complaints. When Phil became aggressive and critical, she would reject him with a cold indifference that cut him deeply. Phil would boil over into a full-blown rage and then would withdraw into being a victim.

Phil and Donna felt locked in an intractable dilemma. Phil had wanted Donna to act as a traditional homemaker like his mother. He knew nothing of compromise, only fighting and conflicts. His view of relationships came from observing his authoritarian father dominating his mother. He wanted the same authority but was troubled with self-esteem issues. Phil and Donna were unable to connect, and neither one knew how to communicate their needs and wants to each other. They alternated between hopelessness and fruitless attempts at reconciliation. When Phil lost his job, Donna lost her husband as the breadwinner and, along with it, her respect for him. She felt abandoned again, and her anger toward her abandoning father resurfaced in her present relationship. Their fights were ugly, with them hurling insults at each other and then retreating into a fuming withdrawal. After the storm calmed they would come together and share their feelings.

How were Phil and Donna to get out of this mess? There were many concepts, insights, and understandings necessary to revamp their conflict style so they could use conflict productively. They were operating from antiquated systems that were tearing away at the fabric of their relationship. Understanding their negative process and how to communicate effectively was a major challenge.

The first thing we did together was to debunk their idealized, romantic fantasy of what the relationship "should be." Then, they learned more about what was hurting them and that they were trying to communicate through their hurt feelings and entitlement to rage instead of more feeling-based expressions. We defined their feelings and what it was they wanted emotionally from each other. We looked into family issues to understand how they were being played out in the current situation. Then, they made agreements about what they needed to do to make the relationship work for each of them, like taking time-outs and talking about how they felt instead of blaming. Because they loved each other and wanted the relationship, they stuck to those agreements. Next, they worked on communicating their wishes for the future and saying simple things such as, "When you take a shower, could you hang up the towel?" They worked on active listening skills, such as, "I hear what you're saying, that it makes you feel that I care about your needs when I pick up after myself." They learned more about compromise, the importance of empathy, and how it's important to

express complaints without criticizing or bla'
needed to dialogue about what kind of life the
other and how they were going to make that h..
my lead of articulating what they were feeling, they ica..
to articulate their deeper feelings and concerns.

Phil and Donna began to understand how they had lost the ability to empathize with each other. They learned to work together to resolve problems and create a new relationship crucible that they could live with. A relationship crucible is a vision for the relationship that both people believe in. It's a road map to actively create happiness that the couple can reference. The map they fashioned was unlike any other but contained what was important to each other, including agreements about how to communicate hurt feelings and needs. The process they created was love-making.

The Confluence of Pain

Working with couples provides a bird's eye view of how we have experienced relationships throughout our lives. What I often observe with couples in conflict is what I refer to as the confluence of pain. What this means is that each person's personal wounds from their experiences collide with the other's. Personal wounds are created from our reaction to being abused by those who were responsible for our care. If we were consistently criticized, rejected, physically beaten, sexually abused, neglected or abandoned, these experiences will generate pain. This pain forms into emotional wounds so that if anyone touches them by being critical or abusive or neglectful, our defenses are quickly marshaled for protection. Typical defenses to personal pain are deflection, shutting down, withdrawal, and/or angry outbursts. Couples who are experiencing intense conflict are often responding to the confluence of each one's personal pain generated from their emotional wounds. How each person's pain mixes with the other's during conflicts is what creates a combustible confluence.

For instance, if a woman felt as a child that she was not interesting to her father and she marries a man who has trouble expressing his feelings because he was punished for having them, this

Love-Making

d be an instance of the *confluence of pain*. These recent or past
unds that were inflicted through the years beginning at an early
ge and continuing on throughout our lives are at the heart of most
confluence. If one partner grew up never feeling valued, and the
other grew up experiencing constant criticism and coldness, they
will mutually fly into an orbit of anger when either one experiences
criticism or withdrawal. In this way early wounding experiences
are intertwined with each other in a negative way. Another example
might be that one person felt invisible and the other abandoned. So
when one of them feels invisible they withdraw which makes the
other one feel abandoned. This would be a confluence of pain and
might cause a battle that could be quite painful and wounding.

For some couples, instances of requesting love and romantic
reassurances will be met with resistance, which will trigger their
wounds and the pain that it evokes. This hurt will then be converted
into anger and other defenses that will further alienate the other
person. This is why self-knowledge is so critical to love-making.
If we are unaware of the nature and origin of our wounds, we will
also be clueless as to the way these wounds will be enacting protective measures in the form of defenses. These defenses cause people
in relationships to argue incessantly about issues that have nothing
to do with what's really bothering them (remember the toothpaste).
It's exhausting to keep arguing about issues that cannot actually be
resolved.

Betty and Joe

Joe's mother was distant and emotionally unavailable. He had
to constantly be in tune with her for signs of withdrawal so he could
try to prevent it. She insisted that he do what she told him, and her
controlling presence was a great source of frustration. He never felt
truly loved by her.

Joe's wife Betty came from a family where she felt pressured
to be perfect and do things right or there would also be a loss of
love. She learned to protect herself by doing solitary and soothing activities like reading or gardening. When she did this in her
marriage however, Joe felt that she was uninterested in him and

silently brooded with anger. He would turn his pain into a list of grievances and then yell at her in an angry and superior tone. What Betty heard was that she was inadequate, and Joe in turn felt invisible and unloved.

The confluence of their personal wounds was symmetrical and impossible for them to see clearly. They understood very little about the effect of their early family life on their current conflicts. The interesting quality about this confluence was that it had less to do with each other and more to do with their inner lives of which they were quite unaware. As they began to see what was happening inside, each was surprised.

As they started to work in earnest and looked at all the ways that they could communicate with each other through their wounded inner worlds, they learned how to avoid blaming each other. Betty learned to express her needs for solitary activity in a way that Joe would not take personally, and Joe learned that his feelings of isolation and loneliness were not about Betty. Once they understood what they were actually fighting about and how their pain was interacting, they could more easily resolve their conflicts.

The "Happy Couple"

Jim and Lorna first met while on vacation at a sun-drenched paradise. Within a few months they were married. Jim was Lorna's dream man, and he felt just as strongly about her. Their history tells the story of their conflict. Lorna was the perfect child. She took care of her other siblings and believed that her only way of getting acceptance and love was to be selfless. The cost of her selflessness was that she kept her neediness private and was unable to talk about it. In her childhood she developed a romantic ideal as to how life would be when she found her mate. Her fantasy man would be strong, responsible, and could take charge.

Jim was raised by maids and nannies as his parents were frequently travelling. Consequently Jim never had to be responsible as a child. Jim never learned how to express himself or how to work through problems. When they were home, Jim's parents rarely if ever discussed feelings, morals or values with him. Jim's romantic ideal was that the woman should be quiet, demure, sweet, and caring. He believed that as long as he brought home the money, he was fulfilling his role as a man.

After their first child was born, Lorna noticed that Jim seemed unsure of himself. He had problems doing odd jobs around the house and when he encountered any difficulties, he withdrew. It was not long before Lorna began to berate Jim for being lazy. She was angry that he had fooled her into believing that he was so capable when he wasn't. Lorna took it all very personally. She believed that he wasn't helping out because he didn't care about her.

Jim and Lorna entered therapy with a host of complaints. They mostly revolved around her notion of what her husband should do if he loved her. She wanted him to be more active and take charge and "know" what to do. She was critical and contemptuous of Jim. He was frustrated and didn't feel that he could do anything right. "Nothing I do makes you happy," he would cry out in frustration. She would counter, "Well, if you would open your eyes, you would see what needs to be done instead of being a lazy slob."

Jim came to the sessions depressed and sullen. He sat with tears running down his face while Lorna criticized him. Lorna was trying to pressure Jim into changing, using her anger and criticism, and it was not working. He was totally shut down.

We began by defining what it was that Jim and Lorna were feeling. Jim was deathly afraid to tell Lorna that he didn't know how to do many of the things she wanted him to do, for fear of her criticism and withdrawal. He was also depressed because her criticism was too much like his criticism of himself. He believed that if he were to let her know how he felt, she would leave him. Lorna began to understand, which gave Jim the courage to express his feelings.

As Jim and Lorna began to talk about their values and beliefs, they realized that they were on the same wavelength but had not worked out how they were going to help each other. The reality was that Jim didn't know how to express his needs or fears and had no idea how to work with Lorna to divide some of the tasks that needed to be done. Lorna's constant criticism only served to increase Jim's feelings of inadequacy. Secretly, he felt Lorna was right—that he was useless. To cover his bad feelings about himself he withdrew, which only made Lorna angrier and more convinced about how right she was. Lorna may have had some valid reasons for feeling the way she did, but instead of being able to talk about them with Jim, she felt hurt and retaliated with criticism. They established what they valued. What eventually came out was that Lorna was using the defense of being "right" to ward off her fear of getting close and being found out to be less than perfect herself. She was afraid Jim would leave her if he found out how "bad" she really was.

Jim and Lorna defined their values and beliefs and found new means of connecting. Once they could do this, they started getting along much better. When they could both see that each one's idealized expectations were the cause of many of their conflicts, they began to have a healthier and happier relationship. When they could behave in ways that promoted love instead of squelching it, they were able to allow the love they felt to come out in a safe environment.

For love to grow we must create an atmosphere that enables it to thrive. There are some essentials that help keep couples focused on what's necessary for love to develop and expand. One of those essentials for love-making is to accept, even forgive, our parents. In this way we take ultimate responsibility for the outcome of our own lives. As we allow ourselves to define our own destinies, we both separate and become true individuals. In this way we cease blaming others for our own misfortunes. We can truly take the wheel and put our lives in our own hands.

Melanie Klein, who worked closely with Sigmund Freud and contributed many classic works to the field of psychology, wrote:

A good relation to ourselves is a condition for love, tolerance and wisdom toward others. This good relation has, as I have endeavored to show, developed in part from a friendly, loving and understanding attitude toward other people, namely, those who meant much to us in the past, and our relationship to whom has become part of our minds and personalities. If we have become able, in our unconscious, to some extent to clear our grievances toward our parents, and have forgiven them for the frustrations we had to bear, then we can be at peace with ourselves and be able to love others in the true sense of the word.

The words of Melanie Klein ring as true now as when she wrote them so many decades ago. She goes on to say that:

Part of the process of loving someone is to make peace with ourselves, our history, and our upbringing. To find those inevitable similarities and differences is the beginning stage of relating to another person without losing who we are and what is truly essential about us. How love is made not only involves how we behave toward our partner but how we are toward ourselves. How can we love someone else when we have no love to give?

Melanie Klein speaks to what it means to love someone from the inside out. The better our relationship is with ourselves, especially because we have resolved our self-esteem, self-criticism and self-disapproval issues, the more capable we are of loving someone else. Love that lasts begins with self-acceptance.

2

Intimacy and The Art of Love-Making

The married are those who have taken the terrible risk of intimacy and, having taken it, know life without intimacy to be impossible.

Carolyn Heilbrun

The word intimacy originates from the Latin word *intima*, which means "inner" or "innermost." Thomas Patrick Malone writes in *The Art of Intimacy*, "The outstanding quality of the intimate experience is the sense of being in touch with our real selves. It allows us a fresh awareness of who, what, and how we are."

For most of us the word *intimate* conjures up romantic images of candle-lit dinners, slow dancing, and long passionate kisses. Romantic gestures are certainly a dominant theme of intimacy, but there is more. Intimacy is actually the result of expressing our feelings and personal secrets to each other. Intimacy is our response to feeling deeply cared about, loved, and accepted. To be loved for our own sake, warts and all, brings with it a sense of intimacy.

When we share details about our life that usually remain hidden, we are connecting in an intimate way. The extent to which we can disclose deeply private personal feelings and experiences is proportionate to how safe we feel. What intimacy means to each person may vary and even change over time. It can be linked or entwined with sexual closeness, but not necessarily. In addition to sexual encounters, intimate feelings are produced from shared moments of emotional connection. Intimacy is the product of relationship work and is the result of feeling emotionally connected to our loved one. It's the operating principle for love-making.

Ideally, intimacy is a blend of emotional closeness, spiritual connectedness, and openness. Intellectual collaboration and familiarity, especially with one another's culture and interests, forms the basis for friendship and intimacy. It may also involve shared religious or philosophical beliefs and a genuine appreciation of each other. Finally, intimacy is an emotional response to knowing someone well, by virtue of shared experiences.

The most powerful and profound awareness of who we are occurs when we open our hearts to another, allowing them to touch our deepest sensitivity. To love someone is to appreciate ourselves. In the act of risking our tender inner world, we become more of who we are because we feel touched in an untouched place. Intimacy takes courage because we must risk expressing our deepest sense of self to create it. Love is the result of intimate activity. It reaches into our hearts and we feel satisfied, because love is our emotional food. It is the antidote to painful aloneness. Our ability to establish and maintain nurturing, intimate relationships is not only emotionally gratifying but ultimately helps keep us sane. Most of us are apprehensive about opening our hearts and minds to another for fear of being judged or rejected. Intimacy offers a world of opportunity for emotional connectedness and contentment.

Our survival as a species and as a world demands that we seek connections with others. Intimacy breaks into our isolation and intertwines our souls and if done with tenderness and care, creates safe and secure attachments. What distinguishes us as human beings is our ability to intimately connect with others. Intimacy is the backbone of civilization and is crucial to our continued existence. It is a response to feeling known and loved *because* of that knowledge not *in spite* of it.

Psychotherapy and Intimacy

An aspect of psychotherapy that dates back to Freud, is to bring what is unconscious or unknown to consciousness, that simply talking about our inner feelings and thoughts changes how we feel about them. Bringing what is a "primary process" or unknown or unconscious to a "secondary process" or consciousness, changes how we experience those feelings. Freud and his colleague Josef Bruer were credited with what they called the "talking cure." They discovered that talking had a profound effect on people. When their patients were allowed to "free associate" and talk openly about their feelings, fears, and shame, they seemed to improve.

The primary direction of the initial stage of psychotherapy is to create a safe and therapeutic intimacy. While therapeutic intimacy is a one-way street (therapists usually do not disclose their personal experiences), it's a safe environment that helps to form the beginnings of an intimate process that the patient can at some point take out into the world. In this way they can have an experience that bridges the gap between never-before and what-maybe-possible-in-the-future. The work in psychotherapy is to create an environment that allows deeply felt personal issues to be talked about without judgment or criticism.

Another goal of psychotherapy is to bridge the chasm that our society creates when it loses its ability to nurture its children and emotionally support its population. What psychotherapy can do for people is to help them understand who they are and help them to learn how to create positive relationships. The therapist builds a safe intimacy by creating a nurturing, caring, empathic, and compassionate environment much like a surrogate parent. If we did not have the benefit of close relationships early in life, we will have difficulty with intimate attachments later on and therefore may need to consider therapy. Many people who come to therapy believe that they're inadequate, unlovable, and worthless, when in reality they simply lack the necessary skills and experience needed to interact in the world with others.

Two Horns of the Same Dilemma

There are two major components to feeling intimate. First there is personal intimacy that comes from being familiar with our inner truths, having to do with our dreams, beliefs, feelings, thoughts, wishes, and desires. Second, there is the need to bring this personal process into our primary relationship. This model for relationship intimacy includes emotional availability, responsiveness, empathy, care-taking, the ability to be responsible (even tender) and being able to bear ambivalence during difficult times. How we are with ourselves and how we relate to our partner is a critical part of the dance between our internal and external worlds that either encourages or inhibits our ability to be intimate.

Bringing two people together into a loving process requires that we combine our knowledge of ourselves and our partner. As couples develop a language for their relationship by expressing feelings and thoughts, they meld their two separate worlds into one whole. It's especially helpful to know who we are and who we are *with* during arguments and discussions.

Intimate activity can take many forms, from giving each other the freedom to explore individual interests, to developing mutual values, hopes, and dreams. Intimacy that is created from an open dialogue about our internal and external world ultimately teaches us about ourselves and who we are as a couple. Connecting with each other through interpersonal truths is what creates comfort and solace. To reveal our true self in the presence of another, if done with care, can be enlivening, enlightening, and joyful.

A loving relationship arises from attending to our own thoughts and feelings and to those of our partner. From this process we produce shared values, beliefs, feelings, and interests. What can be more satisfying than understanding with greater compassion because we know someone better? But to achieve this kind of contentment both in our relationship and with ourselves involves a progression of understanding. It is a process, not a short-term goal. There is no actual arrival; there is merely moving further up the same stream. Inner and relationship harmony is achieved from shining insight into dark places, and with that light removing obstructions that block our ability to love.

Long-Term Love

As we attempt to understand long-term relationships, there are several factors to consider about what it takes to make them work over time. Expressing what is in our heart, with compassion, empathy and a willingness to listen are some of the most fundamental processes of intimate love. But there are other factors that impede our ability to love deeply. First, we all fear loss, death, abandonment, and humiliation. Second, we defend against those conditions. Third, the greater the pain that's associated with loss and humiliation, the greater the defense will be.

Our mind automatically creates defenses that will even distort reality to protect us from pain. Defenses are like an odorless, tasteless gas that can color our psychological point of view to create states of mind where others may appear highly attractive and available, or stale and lifeless. Our defenses work to protect us. They may no longer be needed for protection, but we may not always understand that. So, distinguishing what our defenses are doing enables us to short-circuit their effect if need be. To recognize that they can make us critical, angry, reactive, mean-spirited, depressed and moody helps us not to take it out on our partner. The survival part of our brain will do whatever it takes to protect us from the possibility of being hurt, especially if it reminds us of an earlier trauma.

But there is a way for couples to communicate about fear that can strengthen their connection. When people become fearful, they may direct it outward by criticizing and blaming their partner for what they are experiencing. This causes an emotional disconnect. For example, I was working with a couple who were contemplating having another child. The husband criticized and blamed his wife for their money problems. She responded by feeling angry and hurt. Instead of telling her how afraid he was, he defended by criticizing her for spending too much money and being generally irresponsible. She would shoot back with a criticism about his inability to make money. This would create angry and bitter interchanges. He began to see that his criticism of his wife was actually about his fear of abandonment and that having another child might mean he would lose her. He finally marshaled his courage and told her that he felt another child would erode their marriage just as they were getting some time to themselves after the birth of their first child. Once she knew what was bothering him she felt more loving and less angry. She agreed that they needed to make their relationship a top priority if they were to have another child. She deeply wanted more children so they would have a happy family life with children and grandchildren around them. This couple's defenses against their fears of loss were clouding their ability to connect.

Exploring what our defenses are telling us builds a bridge to each other. We need to make a distinction between our fears and our defenses. In this way we can stay in touch with our deeply felt personal truth. It is truth, after all, that is honed from communication and loving insight. This is the dance of intimacy.

How Intimacy is Made

Creating intimacy is much like building a house: it starts with a solid foundation of truth, acceptance, and reality, adding the rooms of our desires, fantasies, wants, and needs, stationing the windows to our soul, wiring in our emotional connections, adding the hardware of values, joy, and sexuality, and joining them all together to create a home. If we are intolerant, selfish, or mean, there will be no lasting intimacy or love. On the other hand if we are caring and kind, the reaction we get will most often be respect and love. To forge a relationship that works requires building both a personal and relationship identity. This identity is a construct that we craft from a dialogue about what we want, need, and what we value about ourselves and our mate. Intimacy is based on knowing who we are and what we want from life together and making agreements based on realistic expectations about core values.

Points of Intimacy

- Understand your fears so they don't show up as blame or criticism.
- Acknowledge first what your partner is telling you before you make your point.
- Discuss what you want and need from each other.
- Build commonality through conversations about deeply held beliefs.
- Air complaints on a regular basis. Don't let them build up too long.
- Listen to your defenses so you know what they are doing.

- Check out your assumptions and ask about them in the form of a question.
- Show respect, be civil, and listen with an open mind.

Listening—the Door to Intimacy

One of the most important things we can do to develop intimacy is to learn how to listen well to what our partner is trying to tell us. Feeling heard and deeply understood is the dynamic form of intimate behavior. Active listening is not only about hearing what our mate has to say but giving feedback that validates what was said. Nodding and saying "Uh huh," and repeating back what we heard are all active responses. It's this ability to let our partner know that we appreciate what's being said that helps create closeness even during conflicts.

Mirroring is the best method for active listening. This skill may sound something like, "You must feel terrible about what your boss said to you." When in doubt, mirror. It's a great method of actively listening and is often an end in itself. Offering solutions doesn't work unless we are specifically asked for them. When our partner is telling us about their bad day, it is probably not the best time to explain why we think they're having one.

Many conflicts escalate because neither person is listening to what's being said. Active listening is about active empathy. Empathy is the center of active listening. Empathy is putting ourselves in the other person's shoes or seeing things through their eyes. Heinz Kohut developed a school of psychology referred to as Self Psychology. He defined empathy as "vicarious introspection," which is the ability to vicariously imagine and feel the experience of the other. True empathy is a bridge to the mind and heart of the other. The most common mistake that couples make is to miss the emotional component in a discussion or a conflict. Empathically tuning in to the sounds of the heart is what it means to actively listen.

The Road to Intimacy

- Discuss and define realistic expectations.
- Make time to talk and include hopes and dreams.
- Ask about your partner's day and how he or she is.
- Think about what you want to say so your partner will hear it.
- Talk about fears, concerns, and worries.
- Explore what you can do to help your partner with the things that are important to him or her.
- Help create new solutions to old problems.
- Pay consistent attention and show respect to each other and the relationship.
- Express regular physical affection.
- Make eye contact during discussions.
- Experience excitement and fun together.
- Promote psychological, physical, and emotional safety.
- Think of some spontaneous surprises.
- Be willing to express caring and tenderness.
- Create a regular time alone together with no distractions.
- Make time to work through anger and resentments.
- Ask for what you want.
- Be honest and express your truth with compassion.
- Promote interdependence and mutual interests.
- Take responsibility for your part of relationship and personal problems.
- Work through family issues and understand how they impact your relationship.
- Stop and listen to what your partner thinks and feels.
- Live in the present and promote a positive future together.
- Emphasize positive solutions to life's problems.

- Write a love letter expressing all the things that you love about your partner.
- Write a letter of apology for all the things that you have done to hurt him or her.
- Trade letters.

Intimacy is greatly improved as we develop a deeper bond of shared core beliefs. Fashioning agreements about moral and ethical behavior creates a secure base. When couples know what the rules are, it's possible to safely walk through the minefields of potential conflicts by being aware of when and where not to step.

Examples of Core Ethical Beliefs

- I will not lie, cheat, or steal.
- I will do unto others as I would have them do unto me.
- What I say I will do and what I do will be the same.
- I will behave toward others in a way that makes me proud of myself.

The Full Range of Human Emotion

Intimacy stimulates an entire range of feelings and moods. In healthy relationships, feelings may fluctuate between being in love, to not much feeling, to downright annoyance or anger. These levels oscillate depending on the vagaries of life and internal or external conflicts. Life stresses such as work pressures, health issues, family crises, difficulties with friends and more, affect our mood states, evoking emotional responses. If we are to live in harmony with our partner we need to be aware of how our moods and feeling fluctuations affect our relationship.

Mood changes within a relationship are not necessarily indications of psychological ill health. Troubling life issues stimulate our emotional memories, thus creating our moods. *There is no cure for life.* We will all experience death; we will all have physical infirmities, losses, and painful remembrances from our past. Relationships function well when there is a mutually shared reality. This reality means that couples understand how their moods and character traits affect their ability to love each other and that they also accept that some of those blocks occur naturally. Developing an awareness of the variations in emotions from day to day helps us to form realistic expectations for our relationship. We cannot always be cheery and fun-loving. At times we are all plagued by dark moods and anxious moments. If this becomes a part of our knowledge base, we can provide a space to work on it instead of taking it personally.

What We Can Do About Those Fluctuations

- Sometimes the best thing to do is nothing; just let the mood pass.
- Be available to listen when your partner wants to talk.
- Give your partner space to work through his or her mood.
- Include feelings and moods in your dialogue with each other.
- Learn to make room for both of you in your discussion.
- Be conscious in plain sight. Be as transparent as possible.
- Live and let live.

Boundaries? What Boundaries?

What do boundary issues have to do with intimacy? Generally, boundaries refer to interpersonal space, which can be either physical or emotional. Physical space means how much physical distance and alone time we need for our well-being. Emotional space is about being able to express what we need and want both individually and with our mate. Boundaries are derived mainly from feelings. Feelings tell us what is uncomfortable or pleasurable. We learn how to understand what our feelings mean from our parents. Children are then able to set boundaries from information that parents give them about how they feel. From these consistent interactions they establish an emotional vocabulary that enables them to express feelings and set boundaries as adults. If this is not done early on, they will have difficulty establishing boundaries later in life. This is one of the most common reasons why people cannot tolerate intimacy. If we have no way to vocalize our need for physical or emotional space when we need it, then it would make sense that we will become claustrophobic when our partner tries to get close.

We naturally feel like moving closer if someone feels comfortable; we tend to move away if it doesn't. Being passive, distracted, creating conflict, devaluing or working long hours unnecessarily as a way to not deal with issues, are some of the ways we set boundaries if we cannot articulate what we need to our partner. In his song "50 Ways to Leave Your Lover," Paul Simon opines, "Get out the back, Jack / Make a new plan, Stan." This is the feeling that comes over us when we can't establish proper physical or emotional boundaries.

Most individuals have their own fixed preferences about personal boundaries, but it takes some processing with our mate to agree on boundary issues within a relationship. Frequently in the early stages of romantic life, couples are joined at the hip. The initial intensity of desire and fear of loss binds them physically together. After some time, they begin to feel the need for some physical or emotional space to engage in personally satisfying activities. This requires the ability to both sense the need for it and the ability to articulate it.

Some Theories on Boundaries

Devaluation is one of the most effective defenses for gaining physical and emotional space. If we inwardly and outwardly devalue our partner, then we are actively creating the distance we need. To devalue is to diminish our dependency needs and protect us from the fear of intimacy. The less our partner is worth to us, the less we have to need them and the more space we create. Most people have no idea that devaluation is a defense and is meant to create a boundary because they have no words to describe how they feel. This is the unfortunate thing about devaluation; it's invisible to the person doing it. Discussion about boundaries can help couples bypass potential conflicts. This communication helps establish firmer and healthier boundaries. Boundary discussion often serves the purpose of actual boundary formation. There is no buzzer that sounds when a boundary has been crossed; we have to understand what boundaries mean, both within ourselves and between each other, to create a sense of safety.

Practical Solutions for Boundaries

A positive means of setting boundaries would naturally include some clarity about our feelings, needs and wants and what feels right for our partner. To be true to ourselves is to be true to our own personal space. Compromises need to be made, and finding the spot where each person feels comfortable is the eventual goal. Boundary issues may include feeling pressured for connection, affection, sex, or intimacy when we don't feel ready for it. If we cannot establish a way to communicate our needs to each other, then we may risk violating a boundary. When we step over our partner's boundaries, we may find them in a fight-or-flight reaction, and an argument or distance will result. If we can't say no when we need to, then it will be difficult to be close for fear of losing oneself altogether. If we set boundaries on a regular basis, we feel more comfortable. If we're not sure what we feel or how to express our needs, we may need some help to develop our internal vocabulary.

Examples of Boundary Statements

- I need some alone time.
- Could you please let me know when you aren't feeling close to me?

- Would you please let me know when you want your space?
- I'm not feeling well; I need you to help me.
- Please tell me what you want instead of sulking.
- Please ask me if you need to borrow my tools.

Finding a Home on the Range

Jon's wife Joan owned several horses, and whenever she could get away she would go out to where they were boarded. Jon grew up on a ranch with horses and rode every day as a boy. To him horses were a mode of transportation, adventure, and fun. Joan had bought her first horse as an adult. She loved riding, training, grooming, and attending horse shows. On one particular Saturday, after a long and difficult week, both were feeling tired and edgy on their way out to the ranch. Jon's agenda was to go on a trail ride and chill out. Joan wanted to do chores that involved working around the stalls. When they arrived she promptly read him her list of things that had to be done. By the time she had read six of the items Jon could feel himself getting tense. Wanting to be a good sport, he went along with her agenda, but inside he was seething.

As Jon and Joan were driving home, she cautioned him to slow down as there were dogs in the area that could run out into the road. He replied tersely that she was picking on him. This triggered a defensive reaction from Joan, and they began to argue. Jon had come to relax and instead, there was tension. What were they not seeing?

They sat quietly for a while and when their anger subsided, Jon acknowledged his agenda, his fatigue, and his inability to talk about it. Joan talked about her stress and her need to get so much done. They tried to understand what their basic conflict was about. Jon explained that he was especially sensitive to the way she asked him to do things. He discussed how her intensity was difficult for him when he felt stressed. The unraveling was crucial.

Jon's father could be insulting and very controlling. During his childhood his father often ordered him around. Jon felt controlled and pushed around by his father, so when Joan told him what to do, it opened an old wound. Not only did his father never take the time to explain to Jon what his feelings were telling him about what he did and didn't want, but he also never allowed Jon to express his feelings at all. So here he was at the ranch, having a very difficult time laying out his boundaries to Joan and because he couldn't do it, he got angry.

Joan thought he was being very reactive, and she hadn't understood him. Her intention had only been to get some work done. Joan also grew up feeling very controlled. Now as an adult, the ranch was her place to be in charge. She was unaware of how her behavior affected Jon. As they began to understand what was going on, many of the complex underpinnings of this conflict became clear. Jon reacted badly to being controlled or ordered around and was having difficulty setting his own boundaries.

They processed their needs and complaints, and their boundaries became more transparent. They felt safer and therefore more intimate. The key factor was their willingness to calmly and thoughtfully go through their experience together until they found a solution.

Intimacy Was Preserved Because

- Neither one withdrew, was critical, defensive, controlling, or became contemptuous.
- They listened to each other until they understood each other's position.
- They went deeper to see the source of the pain.
- They made a plan for next time.
- They concentrated on their mutual wants, needs, and feelings to define comfortable boundaries with each other.

Just as intimacy is so critical to making love last, there are equally daunting blocks to our ability to be intimate and to love freely. We will be exploring some of those obstructions in this next section.

Factors That Promote Distance Between Partners

- Inattention to each other and the relationship.
- Lack of respect for each other.
- Little physical contact.
- No eye contact.
- Loss of passion and excitement.
- Verbal, physical, and emotional abuse.
- Too many predictable routines and interactions.
- A lack of tenderness.
- Inability to express feelings.
- Poor conflict resolution skills.
- Not making time to be alone.
- Presence of unspoken or unresolved anger and resentment.
- Unrealistic expectations.
- Avoidance of confrontation.
- Inability to ask for or articulate wants and needs.
- Being compliant and saying what you think your partner wants you to say.
- Deception and dishonesty.
- Game playing.
- Passive aggression.
- Thinking that you can change your partner.
- Being too controlling.
- Blaming, shaming, criticizing, and judging.
- Acting like the victim.
- Being unwilling to look into family issues as a source of current issues.
- Assuming that you know what your partner thinks and feels.

• Not living in the present.

• Being unable or unwilling to work out the past.

• Negativity.

Love brings forth our entire emotional experience, and this would naturally include our personal pain. For those of us who have felt the sting of rejection, loss, or abandonment, loving someone creates a certain amount of distress. The urge to possess the other so we can keep ourselves safe from rejection can border on obsession. The paradox of love is that we want to possess the desire of the other — want them to love us as we love them — yet this same desire to possess them can drive them away. The dread of being abandoned or humiliated will determine whether we can tolerate intimacy or if we knowingly or unknowingly will try to sabotage it. These factors in relationships can kill love or strangle it from within.

Control and Perfection, the Ultimate Power Tools

Carl Jung said, "Where love rules, there is no will to power; and where power predominates, love is lacking. One is the shadow of the other." Being perfect is one way to look at control. Personality control by attempting to be perfect is an effort to control how others see us; it's how we hide our inadequacy. When someone acts like a "control freak," we may not know what may be causing it, but we know we don't like it, and we see it as a negative personality trait. What causes someone to want to control others? Is it really an attempt to control one's own internal life? Can we say that controlling the external world acts as an internal control? If we look at controlling behavior from a logical point of view, we can see that it's meant to keep what feels out of control from going that way. Controlling others is a way to control the fear of falling apart or losing ourselves altogether. Trying to control the outside world is an attempt to stabilize our inner world because we fear fragmentation.

Some Theories About Control Issues

Control issues in adulthood begin with early power struggles that were lost to an overbearing parent, causing the child to feel powerless and invisible. These early losses robbed the child of control. When the parent controls his or her child completely, there can be no equality or true relationship. The child's will is squelched. Their parent's needs have prevailed over their own. It's the parent who must help the child to develop an ability to soothe themselves. If not, this lack of nurturing forces the child into isolation, alone and unable to process anxiety or pain. The inability to process anxiety and pain through with the parent means that as an adult the only option available is control. If we have no internal mechanism for controlling our internal fears, anxiety, or pain, we must exert control over our environment so that we don't stimulate these painful and chaotic states.

Parents who use criticism and withdrawal as a means of controlling their children cause them to come up with the same solution: *be perfect or else.* Perfectionism is a method that all children invent to bring the parent closer. The child is angry with the parent for being critical and distant but will not dare express their feelings because they fear the parent will withdraw further. This causes the child to hold onto their anger. They identify with the critical parent and this combined with their anger evolves into a critical inner voice. This inner aggression then makes it impossible for the child and later the adult to feel self-accepting or able to self-soothe. This inability drives the child to look outside the self toward their parents and others for inner stability. The perfectionist becomes a people pleaser to gain the equilibrium that is lacking within.

Perfectionistic behavior that is intended to create closeness by approval-seeking instead creates distance. The work to be perfect does not allow us to either disclose our true self or to be spontaneous. Every move must be measured against the ideal perfect self. We want others to praise us so we can feel better inside, but the inevitable outcome is alienation. The drive for perfection pulls us into ourselves to fix what feels defective. We want to make ourselves perfect so our flaws won't show and others won't withdraw from us as our parents did. So our efforts to gain closeness fail because we must focus inward to hide our imperfections and therefore cannot connect with others in a real way. Perfectionism is essentially inauthentic because we must hide our true self in favor of a false self that is sculpted to fit every situation. These behaviors are not bad or wrong; they are intended to get needs met and to maintain internal equilibrium. But they cannot give us what we truly need. When couples encounter perfection and control, it's a clear indicator that they are looking to their relationship to do something that they are unable to do for themselves. We all need to feel accepted but if we try to get others to do that for us, we end up becoming even more cut off and alone. Taking control of our need for self-acceptance allows us to forget ourselves and focus on the other. In this way we can find the kind of quality connection we are yearning for.

Some Practical Solutions for Losing the Addiction

Recognizing if there is a need for control is the first step. The ability to see what each of us needs from others and what we must do for ourselves is the second step. The third step is to understand our history and how it has affected the way we get our needs met. Finally, the last step is to learn how to nurture ourselves. Following these steps can be a good guide for keeping us on track and not overburdening our relationship.

What becomes clear is that people do not decide to behave badly. They do so because they're afraid and are in some degree of emotional pain. Behavior has logic to it; it's about something or it wouldn't be there. The body doesn't lie, it can only feel. One has to think to lie, and the body simply reacts; it just is. It doesn't know how, it just feels. Most importantly, we need to know what our feelings are telling us about what's happening to us. Only then can we find a way to communicate that important information to our partner. The goal is to discover the reasons why we feel as we do and develop a vocabulary for expressing those needs and feelings from the information that our body is sending us about our needs.

We can observe in children what is still true in adulthood, which is how much positive feedback matters. There seems to be an innate tendency for people to react more strongly to negative information than to positive. We are prone to point out the negative and overlook the positive. Conversely, in my years of doing psychotherapy I have witnessed the relationship between painful childhood experiences and current psychological difficulty and I'm continually amazed at how well most of my patients are functioning considering some of the circumstances from which they come. I'm so pleased when I experience their lives improving, and it's mostly due to them feeling cared about, believed in, and in some way loved.

The most significant factors in this discussion about human interactions are the blend between who we are, our history, and how our internal life merges with others. The idea is to balance our precious connection to others while creating a healthy internal life.

Obligation is the Death of Intimacy

Almost everyone is obligated to do things they may not want to do but feel they must. Sometimes we get overloaded with obligations to the point where we become resentful. When our lives are filled to the brim with obligations from work, family, and friends and we believe that we must do what is asked or risk rejection, we may lose our vital connection to who we are. We become a thing instead of a person. To maintain our connection to who we are, it may be important to understand that we do not necessarily "owe" everyone else more than we "owe" ourselves. To this end, *everyone counts, including us.*

There are obligations that are hopefully pleasant but mostly unavoidable like birthdays, weddings, funerals, holidays, religious rituals, business meetings, and regular visits to family. They are a part of life. But too many obligations can overburden us and affect our ability to be generous toward ourselves. Yes, making others happy can make us happy, but more importantly we must strike a balance between what we do for others and what we do for ourselves. To balance personal obligations and our responsibility to ourselves takes some thought and reflection. Personal fulfillment and self-esteem work together. Satisfying needs, wants, and personal obligations brings with it a sense of balance/contentment and self-esteem.

The French existentialist Albert Camus asks "*Why Not Commit Suicide?*" He postulates that if life has no meaning, is absurd, and makes no sense, why live? He ultimately concludes that even though life itself has no meaning, our individual lives can. He stresses that if we do things that we feel passionate about and are interested in, then our lives will have meaning to us. Our responsibility to ourselves is to take care of our body, intellect, heart, and spirit, and to find intimacy with another person so we can receive affection and feel emotionally connected and fulfilled.

One of the basic philosophic tenets of Zen Buddhism is the Art of Selfishness. It's based on the belief that if we are selfish, then we are in the act of making ourselves happy. In this way we give our happiness to all those around us. We must try to find equilibrium between our obligations to others with our need do things that make us feel good about ourselves. Working toward a balanced life is the goal, even if reaching it may be hard to achieve.

So, as we look into intimacy, we come to understand that it's an enactment. It's about activating our heart, our mind, our sexuality, and our indomitable spirit. Woody Allen sums it up in his tour de force *Annie Hall* when he asks, "Why do we want relationships at all?" He tells a story about his uncle, who when asked why he dressed up like a chicken replied, "Because I need the eggs." We need relationships because they are how we get emotionally fed through nurturing and intimacy. We do need the eggs. When we accept that we humans are inescapably bound to each other the same way we have been for thousands of years from tribes to communities to nations, we come to see the value of love and relationships as our very salvation as a people. Intimacy is our life blood; we need it to feel alive and connected to something that makes us feel emotionally content.

Intimacy is the emotional balm for the inescapable entrapment of our own skin. It's our bond with others that enables us to cross over the psychological void of separateness to the world of our loved one in the transitory bliss of connectedness. If we are to be intimate, we must open our heart, knowing that we can be hurt, and give of our precious gift, our tender truth, in a moment of being truly vulnerable and alive. To this end we strive and wish and dream.

3

How Conflict Can Make Love

The love you take is equal to the love you make.
Lennon and McCartney

From Circles to Spirals

Kenneth Cloke, esteemed author and mediator (and my brother), writes in his book, *The Crossroads of Conflict:*

> Most conflicts are filled with a cacophony of noisome chaos that confuses people about their real meaning. Yet at their center, as in the eye of a hurricane, there is silence and peace, which poet Rainer Maria Rilke described beautifully as the "noise at the entryway to the voiceless silence of a true conflict." When we pay attention to this voiceless silence in conflict—to what people really mean—everything they do or say can lead to the center of their dispute. The parties can locate this center, as with all circles, not by moving outward against their opponents, but by moving inward toward the core of the conflict within themselves.

Sparring Partners

We fade in on a couple sitting quietly at Sunday morning breakfast, when without warning a seemingly innocuous comment swiftly escalates into a prodigious conflict.

> ***Her:*** Yesterday when you took out the trash you left a total mess. Are you blind?

Him: I just can't win. Whatever I do is never good enough for you.

Her: Well, if you would just open your eyes and pay attention to what you were doing, then I wouldn't have to say anything.

Him: There you go, blaming me again. You are such a control freak.

So it goes until either they become really angry or stop talking altogether.

All couples experience conflict. Conflict can either be destructive and break the connection or be the basis for deeper intimacy. Imagine the same conflict but expressed in a different way:

Her: I want to ask you something, but I don't want you to take it the wrong way. First, I want to thank you for taking out the trash, but next time could you please check to see if you left any trash behind? I would really appreciate it.

Him: I'm sorry; I was in a hurry and didn't realize that I did that. I will definitely check next time, and thank you for telling me in such a nice way.

In the second dialogue we can see how this exchange brings them closer. First she introduced the subject, then she thanked him, and then she put her request in the future. Here is another:

Her: I know how hard you're working, but when you promise me that you will take care of things and then you don't, I feel unimportant to you, and it hurts my feelings.

Him: You're right; it's thoughtless of me to not follow through. You are really important to me, and I love you. I will try to keep my promises in the future.

If the next time he keeps his promise, it will make her feel that he is making an effort to do something that's important to her.

This is love-making. When our partner feels heard and that his or her feelings matter, it creates a positive feeling. At the very least it will bring the couple closer. The above dialogue represents some of the crucial concepts that keep conflicts from getting out of control. Creating a safe and secure conversation takes concentration, but once the steps are learned, those nagging emotional breaks will only be temporary. The goal of conflict resolution for couples is not only to not inflict any lasting pain, but to feel closer and more loving by the end of the discussion.

What Makes Connections and What Breaks Them?

We all know that kindness, thoughtfulness, concern, and empathy create connections. So, why is it so difficult for couples to behave that way? The simple truth is that the origins of a couple's conflict often run quite deep. Working with couples has taught me that all behavior has a rationale to it, especially when we can get to its source.

I once worked with a couple where the husband was angry and bitter toward his wife for never initiating sex. His behavior was completely counterproductive to what he wanted. As we peeled back the layers we discovered that he felt truly unlovable. Once he understood where his anger was coming from, he could risk expressing how much he needed his wife. This resulted in a deeper bond that led to an improved sexual connection. It just took some digging to ferret out the truth. This little story illustrates the great difficulty couples experience in their quest to have a loving relationship and why it can be so hard to see what gets in the way.

We have all witnessed couples who are quarreling, and their level of criticism, contempt, and defensive behavior makes it clear why they're having trouble. When couples take the gloves off and use words like weapons, they wipe out all the good feelings. We too easily fall into using the same dysfunctional skills we learned in our own family. We then create the same anger and resentment in our current relationship that we felt growing up.

Conflict is the natural outcome of our innate differences, our likes and dislikes, our sensitivities, our perceived slights, and our emotional wounds. These patterns of personality and experience shape the conflict process. Unless we learn how to resolve conflicts we will find the same negative interactions coming back time and again. Each person's sense of reality is based on his or her own unique perspective. We all believe, think, need, care about, are sensitive to, or are wounded by both similar and quite different experiences. These diverse experiences form our personality and worldview. We are born with a certain temperament, physical appearance, intelligence, and innate talents. When we find that special someone, we are encountering a different set of experiences and pre-wired set of traits, all forming their particular personality. Couple conflict tends to arise out of being two different people. We have different childhoods, life experiences, talents and intelligence, and we make different choices. The clashing of these differences leads to natural disagreement. All couples experience conflict. Accepting that conflict is a natural process is the first step toward creating intimacy. It's not *that* we fight, it's *how* we fight. How we respond to conflicts has everything to do with resolving them. Productive and efficient conflict resolution is a vital dynamic in the creation and maintenance of a lasting intimacy.

Jealousy

Erica Jong, who wrote *Fear of Flying*, once said that "jealousy is all the fun you *think* they had." If we think about what breaks our connections with our loved ones, jealousy comes out near the top if not at the very top of the list. Jealousy is as old as life itself. To love means risking loss and hurt. Jealousy springs from loving someone and fearing the loss of this love object. Men and women who fear loss may try to stimulate passions by making their partner jealous. Jealousy is also a factor of self-esteem. When we feel unlovable and undesirable, we may become jealous because we project that feeling onto our mate. Jealousy may also be present when our mate is not open emotionally or does not feel strongly enough about us.

Some jealousy is considered to be a natural part of relationship life. On a more humorous or low-level intensity, jealousy can establish to our partner how important they are to us and how much we love them. David M. Buss, Ph.D., writes in *Evolutionary Psychology* that causing jealousy can achieve several goals for women. It can fortify self-esteem because it's a demonstration of love and devotion, it can increase the commitment of a partner, and it can show the strength of the bond. When jealousy becomes a problem it's because it escalates into anger, rage and conflict. When jealousy breaks the emotional bond between couples it can be a very serious threat to the well-being of a relationship.

The renowned anthropologist Margaret Mead wrote in *Sexual Temperament in Three Primitive Societies* that, "Jealousy is an undesirable, a festering spot in every personality so afflicted, an ineffective negativistic attitude, which is more likely to lose than to gain any goal." Jealousy for most people is reflective of being treated like a possession and feels like distrust.

Envy and poor self-esteem can combine to create a dangerous mix. Envy is based on the feeling that someone else has something we do not. Envy creates an urge to destroy the source of the envy as a way to eliminate it. One can see the potential for violence if the feelings of envy and shame combine to form a rage response. There are obvious clues that let us know whether our feelings are justified or result from shame issues. For example, if we know for certain that nothing at all has happened and yet we are being accused of being unfaithful, we know that the problem lies with our partner. If our partner is keeping an old flame lit and we discover that long, private conversations still occur and the relationship may not be fully finished, it would not be unreasonable to question it. If however, we are continually upset every time our partner casually looks at someone of the opposite sex, we may be projecting our own self-esteem issues onto our partner.

Most people feel inadequate about some aspect of their lives. Our hair is receding, we are too fat, we have a funny looking nose, our penis is not big enough, our breasts are too small or too large, or we have short legs or bad teeth. Maybe we were humiliated at home or on the schoolyard, or someone we once desired rejected us. We go through life with differing amounts of rejection, loss, and wishing for something that never quite comes to pass. We have all experienced desire for someone who does not want us in return. We may have felt humiliated about some family secret or the pain of rejection. It's in all of us to feel some degree of jealousy, inadequacy or envy. Not that it's so bad to feel that way, but more importantly we need to learn how to work through those feelings so that they don't create negative interactions in our relationship.

The Impulsive Couple

Before Brad and Teresa met, they had experienced a wide variety of romantic relationships, all ending somewhat dismally. They were lonely when they met, so their relationship progressed quite fast and soon into it, they moved in together. Teresa was thrilled because she felt she had met "Mr. Right." Brad seemed to love her in the way she had always wanted. He sent love notes, he hung on her every word, and the sex was off the charts. Everything was on track for marriage.

One day, out of nowhere, while they were in a restaurant Brad flew into a jealous rage. He wanted to know why she was flirting with "that man across the room." When Teresa recovered slightly from her shock and dismay, she explained that she was not looking at anyone. They fought bitterly about whether she was flirting or not. She was mystified by his jealousy and reassured him that she had been waiting for him all her life and that she was very content with him. When nothing would convince Brad otherwise, they came to my office for help.

Teresa was already coming to me for therapy, and I knew how crazy she was about Brad. After some discussion with him, it became apparent that his jealousy was about his low self-esteem and fear of loss. Here is a good example of how a shame issue can find its way out of one's inner world and into their present experience. Because Brad didn't feel good about himself, he projected his insecurity onto the stranger in the restaurant. He felt Teresa was so wonderful and he was so inadequate that any man could easily steal her away from him.

Brad began to see that his jealousy and fear were related more to his own insecurities than to Teresa's presumed roving eye. He was afraid to see that his envy, low self-esteem, and abandonment terror were affecting what he thought he saw in the restaurant. Brad's inner conflicts were complex, and it took some time for him to understand how his relationship with his rejecting and critical mother had created a wound inside him that he was now projecting onto his current experience. He was reliving his experience with his mother, except it was in the present. He did not feel connected to his family, especially his mother who frequently had rejected him when he wasn't behaving the way she wanted. Many years later, having fallen in love, those same feelings were haunting him.

Projection works just like it sounds. We project something that is inside us onto a present experience. Internal feelings of powerlessness, weakness, inadequacy, and fear can be projected outward without our even knowing it. What we project onto others comes from painful early experiences that are a part of our unconscious and are therefore held in a safe place. Because the original experiences were too painful for the infant or child to cope with they were split off from awareness. They form a life of their own and when stimulated can burst forth in a display of temper. These same feelings having not been processed properly are loose and chaotic. The pain that is projected seems very real to the person experiencing it. Once the wild and unprocessed internal material can be identified and understood, we have some control over the outcome. If we're unaware of our internal process, we are at the mercy of our own inner turmoil being projected onto our partner. Note: it's not just childhood pain that is significant but all pain no matter when or where in life it's experienced. The difference between infantile/childhood pain and adult pain is that we are usually conscious of adult pain. Early trauma is too intense for infants and children to process or understand, so it's automatically removed from consciousness for psychological survival. There will be more detail in chapter nine, *Shame, Rage and Love-Making.*

Brad eventually understood that he was afraid he would be thrown away by Teresa just as his mother and other women in his past had done. Once he could see how his pain was being projected onto Teresa, he could release his jealousy. Just like a beach ball held under water, his repressed anger had popped up during lunch that fateful day. When his wound spoke, it said to him, *"You are insignificant compared to that handsome man over there."* This wound, although hidden, reared its ugly head when Brad fell in love with Teresa. The residue of early rejection, his resultant self-esteem conflict, and his fear of loss created a powerful jealousy cocktail in Brad. In that moment reality shifted. What had been an innocent, rather casual look around the restaurant by Teresa was perceived as a rejection. Once Brad understood what was really going on, he learned something important about himself. This awareness led to more understanding of who Teresa was so he could differentiate between his fear and Teresa. Brad was able to overcome his jealousy, and they're now married.

The story of Brad and Teresa is a good example of how conflicts, when worked through, can lead to intimacy. The best way to react to jealousy is to investigate our feelings first, so that we can prevent a bad experience from happening in the first place. In this way, we can distinguish feelings of jealousy that are based on a real event from those that are the product of our personal issues. Once we understand the reality, then we can process the problem.

Identifying the source of jealousy is the critical bit. If everything is going well, chances are that if jealousy strikes, it's happening from within us. However, if our mate has a roving eye or there is flirting going on right in front of us then we *should* feel jealous. This would be a good time to be thinking hard about whether we are in a viable relationship with a mature person.

Our Funhouse Mirror

Many conflicts arise out of internal distortions caused by who we believe ourselves to be. These negative images or beliefs are never true. This inner falsification can be understood as a self-esteem or shame issue like feeling unlovable, bad, ugly, inadequate, or weak. This distorted sense of a personal deficit is projected right into most couple conflicts and is often unknown to the person doing it.

Recently, a man came in for therapy with his wife of many years. We were talking about his father for whom he had many times expressed loathing. This time, his wife was the one being critical of his father, and he was defending him. I mentioned that he was being particularly positive about his father, and I had not seen this in previous conversations. He took offense to my comment and reacted as if I was telling him that there was something wrong with him. He instantaneously became angry at his wife and me. I asked him if he felt that I was diminishing him in some way, and he confirmed it. As we began to unravel his distortion we discovered that he felt inferior to both his wife and me, so when I expressed an insight, he thought I was demeaning him. He realized that his feelings of inferiority distorted his perception so that even an innocuous comment was felt to be a put down. He could see that he had behaved that way many times with his wife. He realized that the people he thought were making him feel bad about himself were the same people who loved and cared about him. When he found that it was his own sense of deficiency that he was responding to and that others weren't putting him down, he felt more at ease.

We defend against having our inadequacies exposed and then feeling humiliated, so our defenses automatically arrive to protect us. Our mind and body interact with each other in intricate rhythms of which we are often not aware. The complex interchange between our temperament, our experiences with family members or the lack of it, the life we have lived, and how all of this affects our sense of self is difficult to understand. Grasping how our inner life affects our relationships is challenging. It is, after all, our need to be heard and to connect with our partner that creates harmony. Our personal pain is a message from our past, and if we know what it is, it does not have to disrupt our ability to love each other. The trick is to know about our distortions, so we can make better choices and ultimately control the outcome of our conflicts.

Resolution and Solution

As couples work through disagreements they need to keep in mind some basic concepts that will help them stay on track. The first steps are to develop effective listening skills, practice tolerance, "tune in" to their own behavior and the verbal and nonverbal messages from their partner, and then learn to respond with empathy.

The way our partner reacts to us is a direct result of the manner in which we express our feelings. Interestingly enough, often the message beneath our anger and criticism is almost always positive. We just can't get out of our own way long enough to express our need for love and care. It's so often the case that just under the surface of an angry adult is a hurt child who deeply longs to be seen and heard but only knows how to scream and hurl accusations.

Suggestions for Conflict Resolution

- Do not *defend, criticize, be contemptuous, or stonewall* (John Gottman's *The Four Horsemen of The Apocalypse*).
- Work through conflicts in such a way that stronger values are developed and trust is strengthened.
- Process conflicts with understanding, compassion, and support.
- Soften your message: "I want to tell you something about what I see you doing but I don't want you to take it personally or feel like I'm criticizing you but when we are with other people, I feel like you get so into the conversation that you forget to include me."
- Use conflicts as an opportunity to demonstrate friendship and practice acceptance.
- Make agreements and take them seriously. When your partner can see that you are actively trying to do those things that are important to them, it creates positive feelings.
- The way you respond to a conflict can either reveal your desire for a deeper intimacy or your defenses to the vulnerability of loving and being loved.

What Saved You Then May Be Killing You Now

Children learn coping skills so they can psychologically manage family and peer struggles. The very same skills that helped them to survive emotionally as children may now be hindering their ability to maintain an intimate bond as an adult. If a major coping skill was to tune out family conflict, this same process may be a source of conflict in current relationships. If our family style involved screaming and yelling at each other to help stave off pain, and we employ this same behavior with our mate, it will break our emotional connection. If our parents were tyrannical and critical, we will tend to act the same way toward our loved ones. If we were punished for having needs, then we will have difficulty expressing them.

A major cause of unhealthy couple interactions is directly related to the inability to express feelings and needs. The learned ability to block emotion creates distance between partners. This causes resentment and withdrawal into anger, along with internal and external negative thoughts and behaviors. This dysfunctional process can drive a wedge into the cohesiveness of a relationship. Expressing needs and feelings plays an important role in daily conversation, and from this many disputes and breaks in our connection can be avoided. We can't legislate needs, desire, or even who we love. We know that need-satisfying relationships are the goal. But how are we to be aware if we don't know that we have needs, or what our feelings are telling us, or how to express them? The trouble often lies not only in how we defend against the fear of rejection based on having needs, but also in not recognizing how to express our genuine feelings, wishes, and desires.

The Best Defense—Some Theories for the Theoretically Inclined

Another piece of the puzzle in solving the enigma of intimacy is to identify how our defenses work. The more we know about them, the more effective we will be in neutralizing their effect. What exactly are defenses? Defenses are the way our psyche reacts to the possibility of being hurt. They are built over time from our natural reaction to painful experiences. Defenses protect us from the threat of impending harm. Defenses that arise out of personal wounds are complex and do not change much if at all. The solution is to build a system around our defenses so that we know how to neutralize them when we experience them. This is why appreciating how our defenses work is such an essential part of healthy conflict resolution. The brain creates defenses to protect us from the pain of humiliation. For example, one of the most powerful defenses against feeling inadequate is to create the defense of arrogance and entitlement. This is how our sense of reality is shaped by our inner world. Conflict evokes our entire life experience, especially in close personal relationships. Our self-image is molded from our experience with people we have loved, and it shapes how we respond to the world of others. If our identity was largely formed by tragedy, pain, loneliness, or violence, this emotional information will adversely affect our sense of reality, our ability to love, and how we relate to our partner.

Defenses are typically experienced as denial, intellectualizing, grandiosity, projection, idealizing, and devaluing others, to completely shutting down. The complexity of relationships is compounded by these convoluted defenses. We may not be aware that our defensive argumentative behavior is just like our aggressive parent. Instead we believe we're right, even righteous, which makes us unable to see that we are being destructive or at the very least counterproductive. In these instances, anger is operating to silence the internal message that we are powerless, and turn it back on the other person. This causes us to project our personal issue from our past onto our relationship through the conduit of blame, entitlement, devaluation, and criticism.

Couple Distortion

Let us consider the case of Jim and Sharon. Jim felt inferior and unconsciously feared that Sharon would leave him if she discovered it. Jim's defenses produced a shift in reality as he angrily defended himself and devalued her. He didn't realize that his need to devalue his wife came from his fear of needing her so much. His depreciation of her protected him from certain humiliation and shielded him from his abandonment fears. He did this by criticizing her for being overweight and selfish.

Sharon didn't understand what she did to deserve Jim's contempt. She became sullen, ate too much, went shopping, and was petulant. All of these behaviors only served to fuel Jim's devaluation. As we delved into his fears, he was shocked when he realized that his devaluation and anger were the by-products of his abandonment terror. It was tough for Jim to acknowledge that he felt so negative toward himself, but he did it because underneath it all he could not imagine life without Sharon.

Another function of his contemptuous and critical verbal onslaughts toward Sharon was to weaken her so she would be too fragile to leave him. He would react to a perceived criticism with defensive aggression and come back at her with humiliating language: "You are nicer to our dog than you are to me." After a considerable amount of work, Jim understood that he was communicating his fear of abandonment through his defenses. His wife was perceived to be inadequate instead of him. What astonishing trickery! His mind shifted reality so he could be safe from the horror of once again feeling all alone in the world, all in the service of self-protection.

Acclaimed writer and child abuse expert Alice Miller writes in *The Drama of the Gifted Child*, "*Whatever* we push out of our own garden we find in the garden of our children." We could infer from this that whatever *we push out of our own garden winds up in the garden of our relationship*. This clearly illustrates how critical our understanding of our defenses can be to our ability to maintain intimacy and resolve conflicts.

Finally Jim could say, "I feel like you would run away from me as fast as you could if you knew how much I really need you. So I try to make you feel inadequate so that you will stay with me, and I can feel like I'm important. I'm so sorry that I've hurt you, but I'm trying with everything I have to hold onto you. It's just not a positive way to keep you. Please forgive me." This statement turned Sharon toward him instead of away, and she reached out to him as they turned a negative process into a loving one. This dialogue was Jim's best effort at loving Sharon. The way toward love-making is to comprehend how our defenses are working and make sure this knowledge is a mainstay of relationship processing. Our fear of irretrievable loss, vulnerability, and the belief that we cannot be loved for who we are will create massive defenses.

From my earlier mention of Gottman's Four Horsemen from his book *The Seven Principles For Making Marriage Work*, let me elaborate:

- **Criticism** is often about the fear of being worth less than our partner; it can also be about the inability to express our intimacy fears, hurt feelings, or powerlessness and inadequacy. Criticism is an ineffective way to communicate and almost always brings defensiveness and anger in response. As discussed earlier, the best way to communicate our concerns is in the form of a compliant.

- **Contempt** is the reaction to feeling ignored, uncared for, disrespected, or unloved. It is about some form of betrayal. It mostly comes from the loss of respect and trust from bad behavior. It's about feeling in some way humiliated. Whenever I observe contempt, I see it as a sign that the relationship is in deep trouble.

- **Defensiveness** is usually about not wanting to be discovered as less than perfect. It's related to our need to feel right, respected, or in control. It's a response to being criticized.

- **Stonewalling** is most often is about not being able to get through to our partner. It's a form of punishment, control or manipulation. It can be about the inability to form our thoughts, or the reluctance to express our feelings for fear they will be criticized. It's also a way to shut out the pain of recognizing our own responsibility for a current conflict.

Defensive styles are perpetuated by contempt, defensiveness, criticism, and stonewalling and make it much more difficult for couples to break their negative cycle.

Trusting the Process

Learning methods for disarming our defenses are not simple. One valuable method for seeing what our defenses are doing is to develop a language about them to alert each other when they are being stimulated. Learning about what's triggering our negative responses helps us to steer through the straits and narrows of conflict and strife with less pain.

Also, couples should learn the language of conflict and meaningful dialogue so they understand how to say what they feel and think in a way that is not defensive or critical. If they don't know how not to, then a defense will come up to protect them. Couples who relate in a way that is respectful, thoughtful, and kind will be able to work through their conflicts more easily and at the same time build a deeper intimacy.

Learning to Be True

Learning to avoid our own defenses may sound like this: "I'm not sure why I'm so angry with you this morning; I think it's because you didn't help me last night when I asked. It's still bothering me." Our ability to recognize what we feel helps to find out what's going on so we can begin to resolve it. If we think we shouldn't feel such feelings we're building a wall, while being comfortable with negative feelings allows us to search for their meaning: "Oh, I see why you're so upset. I said I would help you and then got distracted by the television show I was watching; I'm sorry about that." This statement helps to validate the other person: "Thank you for saying that, it's hard for me to know what's bothering me sometimes. I never learned how to do this; my family never talked about feelings."

A generic method for working out conflicts even if we don't agree with each other is to say, "I'm sorry for whatever I may have done to upset you." In this way we're showing that we are willing to listen to what our mate is trying to tell us and acknowledge that we may have done something we shouldn't have. When we understand what we are in conflict about and what our feelings mean, then we can make a plan for how to do it better in the future. One thing we can do is to not assume we have all the information. We need to check out thoughts and feelings first to develop a more accurate view of what our part in the problem might be. Then we can see more clearly how to resolve the issues that we're struggling with.

Double Trouble

Ivan and Eileen were battle-weary when they first arrived for therapy. Ivan would quite calmly point to Eileen's imperfections one by one as if he were pulling wings off a fly. Eileen would explode and run screaming from the room. He would then turn to me and say, "You see; she's crazy." Ivan was calculated, brilliant, and seemed to enjoy setting Eileen off. Eileen was a pawn in Ivan's game. He needed to control her.

Eileen had since childhood dreamed of having a family. She was alienated from her own family and longed for a romantic relationship. She harbored intense, angry feelings toward her father, and they surfaced with Ivan. Her father had abandoned the family when she was young and never returned. Her mother blamed Eileen for driving her father away, and this fostered her rage and shame toward herself and later on toward Ivan. Ivan exploited this situation to keep Eileen dependent.

Ivan was every bit Eileen's match in the rage department. His father was a taskmaster and the role model for Ivan's behavior. Ivan was a lonely and angry child. His father was a tyrant and a perfectionist who demanded that he do everything just so, and when Ivan failed there was hell to pay. Justice was meted out with a sinister and detached coldness. Ivan was terrified of intimacy for fear of being humiliated or rejected. He maintained Eileen's dependency by crafting expectations that she couldn't meet and then through subsequent conflict created a kind of distant connection all the while making her feel crazy. Eileen and Ivan would argue long into the night about who said what to whom. They blamed each other for their negative conflict style. No matter how hard they tried to work through their rage, they clung to their cycle of shame and blame. Ivan calculated his responses, and one by one he would list Eileen's inadequacies and failures. Eileen would fume silently, then in a fury rage at him, "You bastard, you don't give a damn about me!" Eileen and Ivan were mired in their defensiveness and could not comprehend the way that they were poisoning their relationship.

Once they understood that their conflict style was an attempt to form a bond, albeit a negative one, they were able to see more clearly why they were concocting irresolvable conflicts. As they peered around the edges of their rage they truly began their struggle toward intimacy. They came to understand that there was another route to intimacy, perhaps a more emotionally dangerous process of opening up, but one that would eventually be worth it. They found out that there was no intimacy without risk. They glimpsed for brief moments how afraid they were to touch each other with their words. As they began to grasp how their abuse as children had hardened into feelings of hatred for one another, they could feel great compassion for their mutual suffering. It took dogged determination to see what had once seemed impossible to comprehend. Ivan and Eileen were willing to look at themselves differently and to include their early experiences in the way they responded to each other. In this way they created the possibility for a more satisfying intimacy.

The Relationship Paradox

Many couples miss the true meaning of their complaints. While working with a patient, I made what I thought was an innocent comment, but she later phoned me to say that I had been insensitive. I recalled that her husband frequently complained about having to "walk on eggshells" because she was so easily hurt. He reported that when he did complain, she wouldn't listen and would instead become angry. Then she needed him to soothe her hurt feelings in a rather long and arduous process. This tended to wear on him, so he kept his distance. She complained about their alienation but could not connect the dots. She didn't understand why he had turned away from her. After a careful examination of her experience with me, she saw how her need for comfort was being expressed through a conflict style. She could see for the first time how she first denied her need for affection and attention only to find them through conflict. When she could see that her conflict with me was her way of expressing her need for comfort and to be the focus of attention, she was no longer angry with me or her husband. She learned to ask for what she needed, and he was more than happy to give her reassurance when she asked for it.

When couples are in a conflict, there are a number of dimensions of psychological processing going on. How do we address the complexity of emotional content during and after a fight? The first level or *manifest* content is what becomes immediately apparent in a conflict, what we see on the surface—like haggling over what movie to see. We can refer to the deeper levels within our psyche as latent content that emanates from painful experiences. This shame is related to feelings of powerlessness, self-worth, or whether we feel lovable. Looking for the *latent* content in conflicts is the key to finding a resolution. If we don't determine the cause of our conflicts they will remain the same.

Relationship Givens

As we know, relationships do not always run smoothly. There are many factors that influence our thinking, feelings and attitudes as related to gender, race, religious background, temperament, sexual desire, stress, career pressures, education level, personal sensitivities, and values. If we include these differences in our communication style, we can tailor how we say what we think and feel to our partner. If we know that our partner is biased or has particularly tender feelings about a particular subject, we can take that into consideration in the way we speak our truth.

Other elements that influence our communication style are the demands associated with things like the cost of living, work, family, friends, personal interests, and health issues. We cannot help but bring these pressures to bear in our relationships. It's impossible to shield ourselves from these stressors. Couples who fashion their communicative style around a model that reflects this complexity create a healthier partnership and ultimately facilitate a more loving relationship.

The goal of healthy couple interaction is to organize our communication style around the particular needs of our partner. To respond to our partner with tolerance, understanding, and compassion toward differences amidst feelings of fairness, concern, and a willingness to share ideas is the goal. Respect for essential differences creates harmony. Our ability to commiserate with each other by including both our manifest and latent content into our communications helps draw us closer. If we want a safe and secure relationship we need to soften our language so we can enter the inner sensitive world of our partner. Understanding latent content helps us stay in a position of support and nurtures both ourselves and our partner. All this requires focus and time. With all the pressure we encounter in our daily lives, this process presents a challenge for couples who yearn for harmony. Making time to get to know each other in this deeper way is not easy but it can lead to greater intimacy and peace.

The Erroneous Need to Say Everything

Conversely, there are people who feel they must talk every issue through to the bitter end and yet never seem to accomplish what they're setting out to do. Over-processing can be a source of disaffection. Many men are uncomfortable with long drawn-out conversations about the relationship. They are ill-equipped to process out the anxiety and stress that these kinds of conversations require. Dr. Susan M. Johnson is a professor at the University of Ottawa and author of *The Practice of Emotionally Focused Marital Therapy*. She explains that in conflicts, "Women swim and men sink." What she means is that men have a hard time with lowering their anxiety levels, while women are internally geared for stress both psychologically and culturally. The experience of over-talking for men often feels like an attempt at control. Being aware of what must be worked through with our partner and when to let it go is imperative for love-making over the long haul. The wisdom lies in knowing "when to hold 'em and when to fold 'em." Not every negative interaction requires discussion. Sometimes the bad moment will pass quickly because it's just about being in a bad mood or a momentary irritation. The important points, such as how to treat one another, hurt feelings, and the need for respect, are issues worthy of discussion. Being in a bad mood may simply require some time alone.

The Argument

Jack and Darlene were married for six years when Jack came home late from working on a Saturday to find Darlene miffed.

Instead of arguing and being defensive as he would have done when they first came to see me, Jack begged off talking about it and then went to the gym. In the past he would have tried to make Darlene feel guilty by telling her that she was selfish and would have been resentful that she was not more supportive. Jack realized that this was just his way of protecting himself from inner criticism and guilt for having disappointed his wife. Before, he would turn the argument around and blame her so he didn't have to feel guilty or bad. This time he decided to think it through before he spoke to her. While he was working out, he began to dialogue with himself, using his own words to help himself out. Eventually he came up with what he thought she could hear without taking it the wrong way.

Empathy was the key to understanding where Darlene was coming from and why she was annoyed. She had been looking forward to being together; she was hurt that he did not make it a priority to come home sooner. As he thought about it, he realized why she was upset. She frequently had to wait for him to come home late at night from work and never complained. Jack had agreed beforehand that Saturday was their day together. He broke the agreement, and on top of it he was late. Darlene was frustrated because Jack overstepped his bounds with her, and he needed to acknowledge it. When he returned home he apologized for not seeing her position and the tension broke right away. This was a much different outcome than when they first began therapy. The key was to listen first without becoming defensive and see her side of it. Sometimes the best solution is to step back, calm down, and work it through on our own before we start to talk about it. Jack's ability to listen empathically and take personal responsibility for his part of the problem played a pivotal role in resolving the conflict. They used this successful process as a template for future problems.

September Love

Roger and Louise met when he was in his early fifties and she was in her late thirties. They married quickly, and Louise was soon pregnant. She very much wanted a child and saw this relationship as her last chance at having one. Roger was utterly unprepared for the prospect of fatherhood again. He had already raised a family and traveled so frequently for business that he was unsure that he could be available. He expressed fears of aging, loss of physical endurance, and concerns about the idea of raising another child just when his other children were finally grown. He felt that he had failed in his first marriage and was very apprehensive about repeating the same experience.

When Roger and Louise first came to my office, they were in crisis. They would recount the minuscule details of who said what to whom and concentrate on who was right by placing blame on the other one. They were getting nowhere. Roger defended against whatever Louise said to him: "Here I'm working non-stop to support you, and all you do is find fault with everything I do." Louise would withdraw into resentment: "He doesn't see me. He doesn't care about having a family."

Roger was hesitant to come home at night because he felt so inadequate to the emotional demands of family life. Louise was dreadfully disappointed in the man who had seemed to be a pillar of strength when she had first met him. Louise was afraid of relationships, too. Prior to marrying Roger she never had a healthy love relationship. Her father had abandoned the family, and her mother remarried and put her new family first. Louise had felt invisible and unloved as a child. She developed a fierce independence, but deep inside she longed to be cared about and loved. In part that was why she wanted a child. Roger and Louise didn't understand the latent content of their discord.

Little did they know that their clashes were so connected to their family pain. Roger believed that Louise was critical, and she believed that he was emotionally unavailable and inconsiderate. Roger and Louise frequently interrupted each other or flew into rages. They both felt aggrieved. They were casualties of their histories. The pressure of having a child so early in their relationship and their inexperience in managing stress and intimacy made it difficult for them to feel each other's pain. It took quite a bit of work for them to begin to understand the true source of their conflicts. She wanted him to nurture and care for her but could not express it. Instead, she raged, and he shut down. Once he could understand what she wanted, he was more able to respond. The key for him was to recognize that his bad feelings about himself were causing him to shut down whenever Louise expressed disappointment. His attacks on her were actually a defense based on his feeling of being inadequate as a man. He needed that information to be hidden from Louise for fear that she would leave him. Understanding how this latent content was affecting him and what he was doing to protect himself allowed him to listen better to her complaints. They eventually realized that in order to resolve conflicts, they needed to determine the true source of their personal problems and hear each other out. The best condition for working their conflicts through positively was to establish a nurturing environment, one that allowed for dialogue instead of argument.

Getting to the Source of Conflicts

So, how can couples contend with infantile longings and depression when most of this material is out of reach? The truth is that relationships bring everything to the table.

Pop psychologists tell us that simply being truthful is the answer, that "telling it like it is" will solve our problems. With all due respect, "telling it like it is" won't scratch the surface of an intense power struggle that is produced from deep shame or from the effects of childhood neglect. Actions and behaviors such as control, needing to be right, rage, contempt, and hurling invectives at one's mate are more often than not related to more profound internal issues. The problem with self-help is that it's only a piece of the truth, not the whole truth. Many people with more weighty issues feel stymied and defeated with simple solutions. Most of us are not simple. We are complex, and unless we take those complexities into account, we may not get to the core of our issues. This means we may be doomed to repeat the same negative cycle.

Defenses that come up during couple conflicts are quite insidious. What appears one way to the person observing a situation may in reality be something quite different. We may think that we are clarifying ourselves, but we might really be sabotaging intimacy for fear of being psychologically wounded. Let us for the sake of this point describe a man who is scared to death to get close for fear of being hurt. This fear would create anxiety when he begins to feel close. He might pick fights or do things that he intuitively knows will inflame his partner and push her away. Without understanding why, this distance will tend to ease his anxiety. Watching couples behave defensively may seem to the observer to be entirely different than what is really causing the problem. When couples cannot agree on what actually happened, it not only adds to the problem, but obscures the issue that may lie under it.

This need to agree on details leads absolutely nowhere, but couples continue on as if there is a conclusion coming up at any moment. They're really arguing about who is right. It's not going to be resolved; it's circular. I stress that they should stick to the principle, not the particulars of the issue they're discussing. What are they really trying to resolve? The principle of an argument may really be about feeling unloved or uncared for instead of who said what to whom.

The Perfect Blend-Ship

When I ask couples if they would treat their best friend the way they treat their mate, they seem surprised by my question. They hadn't thought of it that way. The ability to treat our mate like we would a cherished friend is the key to keeping our relationship on track. We get respect from being respectful and one of the best methods for receiving respect is by giving it. Giving and getting do not always go together, but giving is the best condition for receiving. Couples who have learned tolerance, patience, and understanding have gone a long way toward creating a lasting love/friendship.

We don't always give friendship its due, but it's an important part of healthy conflict resolution. It's the foundation for love-making. Without it, we can become mired in distrust and insecurity. If we treat our mate like we would treat our best friend, how can we go wrong? If we can remember that we're with a friend when we feel the urge to retaliate, it can help us to take a beat and think about what we're going to say before we say it. It's necessary for relationship harmony to process disunity by being the friend who listens, cares and wants what's best for us. Negative behavior is not a good teacher. Friends also tell us the truth in a way that is kind and compassionate. If we treat our partner like we would treat our best friend it will help keep us on track when we feel angry and resentful. The best condition for doing this is for both people to agree on the goal of being friends and then behave accordingly.

Once, in a session with an argumentative couple whose style of arguing was to bring up what the other one did wrong, I asked a question that stopped them in their tracks. After a protracted argument, I asked, "Have you resolved anything yet?" They both turned to me somewhat relieved that someone had stepped into this cyclical argument and said in unison, "No." The work was to find the real source of the conflict. It turned out that neither of them felt cared about. They had never developed a friendship so they treated each other the way they had always treated other family members. Once they began working on being caring friends they could find solutions that worked for both of them.

What's So Wrong About Being Right?

Accepting our humanity is crucial for healthy conflict resolution. This means that we have acknowledged that our shortcomings, inconsistencies, foibles, and flaws are all part of what it means to be human. To resolve conflicts we must understand that it's more important to be connected than to be right. The Japanese have a term *wabi sabi*, which means the perfection of imperfection. Acknowledging, even embracing our imperfections helps us to eventually accept and own up to them when necessary. What I mean by *embrace* is to allow bad feelings about ourselves to come forward so we can consider how we might change the way we experience them. An embrace allows us access to our emotions and ultimately provides choices as to how we might want to respond. Being aware of how our defenses work makes it possible to choose how we want to express what we feel. For example, needing to be right is often a defense against feeling inadequate or wrong. Being *wrong* means we're bad, stupid, and unlovable. Being *right* means we're good, strong, and therefore lovable. Embracing our need to be right allows us to look deeper. It may not be pretty, but it may save our relationship. The need to always be right alienates our partner, because it means they must be wrong. No one wants to be wrong all the time. *Being right or wrong is of no value in resolving conflicts.* What matters most is what's causing the fight and what we can do to make it better. To embrace our pain is to accept ourselves and brings our personal problems near to us so we can find solutions.

Accepting the Unacceptable

Our lack of self-acceptance can be the source of much contention. It creates defenses like denial, blame shifting, or needing to be right. These defenses make it difficult to see or listen to our mate. Non-acceptance is always projected onto our partner, so what we may see as hostility is actually about deeply held, internal, negative beliefs. Learning how to see more clearly by listening to what our mate is saying to us about ourselves helps us determine what's real and what's not. Mastering the ability to see ourselves through the responses of others will lead us to a deeper understanding of our true nature. *Self-acceptance is based on the internal sense that we are the product of our experience, not the cause of it.* Self-acceptance allows us to take full responsibility for our part of a conflict. We have nothing to prove. No matter who did what to us in our past, it belongs to us now. We are responsible for our well-being, our emotional wounds, and our part in a conflict.

In a therapy session with a couple, the husband kept reiterating his point about his wife's anger. She kept dodging and defending until finally I turned to her and said, "All he wants to know is that you hear him." When she stated that she heard him there was a palpable release of tension and he said, "Thank you." The rest of the session went much smoother. A simple thing like letting our partner know that we understand what they're saying by repeating it back to them in our own words is a powerful instrument for soothing hurt feelings and ending a stalemate. This is an easy way to create connection instead of destroying it. There is always a form of acceptance in acknowledging our partner's feelings and thoughts. That sense of understanding conveys to our mate that what they're feeling and thinking has legitimacy to it and helps to soothe the pain.

The Idealization/Devaluation See-Saw

Stephen Mitchell, acclaimed author, poet, and translator, writes, "What makes someone desirable is idealization, an act of imagination that highlights the qualities that make that person unique, special, out of the ordinary." To be the object of desire requires some idealization, something that makes that person special. Mitchell goes on to say, "Idealizations are the product of artificial sweeteners." When idealizations fail, as they always do, we are left with reality. So, idealizations set us up for a fall. When we first meet someone, we are immersed in idealized fantasy. In the moonlight everything appears to be perfect. As the relationship progresses, idealization inevitably gives way to some disappointment. Eventually that disappointment, if not addressed and worked through, may lead to devaluation, disillusionment, and alienation.

The theory behind idealization goes like this: all infants and children idealize their parents; they must do this to stay attached and neutralize their fear of abandonment. Idealization is also a part of healthy maturation. For example, superheroes and dolls for children are idealized versions of pre-adult identity formation. Idealization can be a kind of saving grace for one's inner fears of abandonment and helplessness. The more unavailable the parent is, the greater the need for idealized fantasy to ease the fears. Rage at the mother and the fear of abandonment must be "split off" from consciousness because expressing these feelings may drive her further away. When, or if, the mother is unavailable for too long, the anger created from the pain of loneliness and fear of abandonment is driven inward and is ultimately directed at the self and later externalized toward others. After repeated experiences of rejection, the child may attempt to be perfect as a means of enticing the mother to come closer and not reject him. In this way the idealized fantasy and the defenses work together.

When the child matures into adulthood and brings idealization with them, it can cause a host of hassles that are based on an idealized view of how relationships should be. It's then that devaluation can rear its ugly head. Idealization and devaluation are two sides of the same coin. Idealization based on the fear of abandonment develops into devaluation for the same reason, to protect us from being hurt. If we devalue, we don't have to care or need someone so much. Early idealizations that keep the fantasy of the mother intact and insure our survival can evolve into romantic visions of a perfect form of love, only to be dashed when reality hits the fan.

Devaluation

Devaluation is the evil twin of idealization. Devaluation also protects us from dependency needs. When we devalue someone we don't have to need them, because we have made them worth less in our own mind. If our needs were rejected in childhood, then we feel ashamed of them and will devalue others to protect us from further pain. Over time, something in this fragile process breaks down, and the devaluation anger breaks out. The anger that is held back from the parents through idealization finds expression in devaluation. An example of personal idealization would be to characterize one's self as need-less, want-less, or self-less.

Idealization is a pure state and cannot withstand imperfection, so devaluation is stimulated when idealization inevitably fails. The failure of our partner to live up to our idealized expectations will ultimately cause them to fall victim to devaluation.

Couples can learn to bypass the trap of idealization/devaluation and instead, express their deeply felt needs for love and affection. To stop devaluation, couples can learn to detect when the signs of idealization and devaluation appear. They can neutralize the effect by defining what they need and want from each other in the moment.

Ways to Devalue

- **Hitting below the belt:** Once you devalue your partner enough you then can feel entitled to hit below the belt both to push away and to establish a safe distance. This process involves using knowledge of the person's soft spots to hurt them. In this way devaluation allows for retaliation and disconnection, the ultimate move to safety.

- **Injustice collecting:** Collecting devaluations is another method of creating distance and safety. After you have internally and secretly devalued your mate for a long period of time you can let them have it all, in one giant explosion. Then you can feel righteous and satisfied that you are right and good and they're bad and wrong. Resentments that build inside and are released during arguments cause contempt and distrust in your partner. Resentments need to be aired as soon as possible. But there is a catch. *If you want your partner to share his/ her complaints with you, then make sure you listen and do not punish them for telling you.* If you become defensive, rejecting, or angry, you are closing the door to communication.

- **Displacement:** Another way to devalue your partner is to make them responsible for your bad day. When you have had a bad day, and the traffic was horrible, or your mother made you feel guilty, these feelings can easily be projected onto your mate. You lash out or become depressed about experiences that have nothing to do with your mate, and yet you somehow feel they are responsible for it.

- **Intellectualization:** Intellectualization is one of the best defenses against the fear of being hurt or being intimate. It can be used as a defense against the fear of abandonment or dependency needs.

We devalue as a way to push the person away, so when we see a blemish or they laugh too loud, a tooth is crooked, or their body is not perfect - we reject them. For the vast majority of people this activity is entirely unconscious.

The Case of Randolph, or *"The Golden Fantasy"*

Randolph was the product of a very distant and depressed mother and a passive father. His mother ruled the household through withdrawal and approval. She was self-obsessed, and his father lacked sufficient definition to give Randy a viable alternative to his mother. He became the perfect child to please his mother. As an adult, he became obsessed with becoming rich and successful. In doing this he figured that he would never need anyone for anything. After he achieved his goal, he began his search for the perfect mate. She would not only be an external source of approval, but in fantasy, she would know how to satisfy all his needs.

Randy was handsome and accomplished at meeting women. He sought out beautiful and well-educated women. He wanted them to be as perfect as they could be. Within a short time, however, when the relationship looked as if it could get serious, devaluation would set in. If his friends did not immediately embrace her, if she needed him, or if she became demanding in any way, she was out. If his friends approved of her, then he would find other ways to devalue her. During his therapy sessions, he let it be known that he kept several women on the back burner while he was involved with his current relationship. His search for the perfect mate drove him toward a perfection that could never be realized. The flurry of dating different women was a way to ward off a depression underneath. The depression was also kept at bay with the hope of finding the perfect mate through his constant search. His pursuit of perfection was a defense against his fear of irretrievable loss. His pursuit of perfection made him continually worry that he was missing out, that there was a more perfect woman out there somewhere. This drove him to seek out new partners in a manic search for perfection. His deeper intention was for a perfect union that would eliminate his abandonment terror and inadequacy, the true source of his pain and the reason for the formation of his idealized fantasy of perfection.

In reality, Randolph was frightened that someone, possibly himself, would eventually discover what he secretly feared—that no one could ever love him or want him because he was flawed. He was caught in an impossible cycle. He feared intimacy, and he feared loss. He was constantly running himself into the ground in his search for perfection. His endless self criticism was both making his search more frantic and depressing him. As we began to understand together how his self-criticism, low self-esteem and fear of loss were driving him to find perfection, his demands started to ease. He realized that even if he found the perfect woman it would only temporarily heal his wound. He found that it was healthier for him to work on accepting himself instead of finding the perfect woman to make him feel adequate.

Randolph was able to make the distinction between his girlfriend Maria and his mother. As he was able to talk to her about his needs and wants, and she with him, their relationship worked much better. The more he accepted his own needs, the less he devalued her. He was finally able to accept that he was someone she could love. As of this writing, Randolph is happily married to Maria, and they have a son, Rudolph.

Responsibility and Consideration

Back in the day when I was a teacher, I discovered that certain standards seemed to apply to most every aspect of discipline. What came to me after careful observation was that two main concepts seemed to cover even the broadest spectrum: *Be considerate toward others, and be responsible for your own stuff.* It seemed to me that the lack of consideration and the inability to take responsibility for one's own messes both internally and externally were at the core of most classroom conflicts. As a therapist, I later applied this to relationship issues. When either person was upset, it generally revolved around the feeling that the other person was not being considerate or taking responsibility for their own actions or the messes they created. Consideration for others and responsibility for oneself and one's commitments are critical to relationship harmony. If we're a good team player, and are able to compromise, we're actively creating a more loving relationship. Consideration is about showing up on time, remembering important events, fulfilling our responsibilities, keeping our promises, and helping when our partner is in need. The definition of responsibility is that we are response-able, which simply means the ability to respond to what our mate is asking of us.

The Power of Humor

Humor is the great equalizer. It aids in diffusing everyday tensions and can end fights before they start. Humor is a conduit for happiness to flow through. A few years back I attended a workshop that John Gottman hosted for therapists. He played a video of a couple who he described as being in a healthy relationship. The couple was discussing money issues, and the whole time they were using humor as a way of dealing with very sensitive subjects. Their ability to laugh at themselves was a healthy way to work out nagging everyday problems while maintaining a positive feeling between them. Developing a style of humor also tends to grease the wheels of reconciliation after a fight or during one. When we can find the humor in situations, it's like saying that "nothing is more important than you are" and not so significant that we can't find the humor in it.

The Theory of Love and Work

Throughout the years of doing couples therapy, certain things that couples do seem to make their relationships run more smoothly. Here are some of the activities in which successful couples engage.

- **Adjusting and adapting:** We need to accept that some change is inevitable and some things remain the same. Successful couples know this. Change is necessary for the continuation of a positive relationship. As we live our lives together, we must allow for change. Feelings evolve, differences emerge, and new ideas and interests arrive. If we allow for these changes and are in an ongoing dialogue about what we want and need, then we're involved in a healthy life process of change. Relationships need to adjust and adapt to remain vital. We simply cannot continue to always do things the same way and expect to create excitement and passion within our relationship. We must continue to search for our personal happiness and to bring this excitement into our relationship so we can love more intensely.

- **Interchange:** Interchange is the process by which couples make time for feedback and problem-solving before small problems become too large to handle. Interchange is necessary for a relationship to function in a more harmonious, creative, and fresh way. Positive interchange about boundaries, values, and interests makes our relationship function better and maintains a vital connection. Healthy relationships afford interchanges that offer perceptive, descriptive, sensitive, and honest interactions of ideas, wants, and needs.

- **Negotiation and compromise:** Negotiation is fundamental to problem solving. What are we willing to give up, and what is too much? The key is to know when enough compromise is enough. Compromise means we get the most important thing we want but not all of what we want. Negotiation is the central working process in a relationship because it relates directly to the different ways we see the world and each other. Negotiating is the method we use to find the spot where both people feel comfortable. Good feelings in our relationship will suffer if either one does not feel that there is a balance between each other's wants and needs. If one person is making all the decisions, resentment is inevitable. Negotiation and compromise are the cornerstones for relationship harmony. Fairness is the guiding principle.

- **Accommodation:** There are critical accommodations that must be made for change to occur. Accepting that change is necessary and allowing for flexibility in making those changes is important to an evolving relationship. Accommodating contrasting ideas about what a relationship is supposed to look and feel like allows for new possibilities. Accommodation is like adaptation but involves another person. Accommodation is the opposite of constraint and ultimately creates change, which facilitates the necessary development of a truly unique relationship. To accommodate and adapt are fundamental processes for the continuation of love and passion in a relationship. Love deteriorates when we refuse to make the necessary accommodations for new ideas and interests.

Accommodating each person's situation and what they want to do with their lives is what forms the character of a loving relationship.

Problem Solving Step-by-Step

Before we can solve a problem, we must be clear about what the problem is. Once we have a mutual agreement on the content—what the problem is—we can create a solution. Then, do the following:

- *When you become angry, take time to cool off.* Anger is a very complex emotion. It's secondary to and is a response to feeling hurt, sad, guilty, shamed or frustrated. Think first about what your partner is feeling and then what it is that you are feeling. Take a moment to think and reflect on your anger, and then consider all the complexities that are present. No progress can be made when you are feeling really angry.

- *Try to determine what's hurting you.* Knowing exactly what hurt you is the first step to resolving the issue between you and your mate. Expressing what it was that hurt you and understanding what hurt your mate while offering a solution is very helpful to resolving future problems. If you can apologize for your part and offer a solution for the next time, you will often eliminate the source of the anger over time.

- *Define what you think the problem is.* State the problem clearly to each other until you both understand and agree: "I think the problem was that you went ahead and made plans without consulting me. It made me feel invisible."

- *Tell your partner what you want.* Why is the situation the way it is? Letting your partner know what you want takes the guesswork out of the relationship. What do you want from each other? What needs are not getting met and how can that be accomplished?

• *Work toward repairing the problem through acknowledging your responsibility.* Solutions involve affirming feelings, and then finding what works best for both people. Empathic listening is the critical aspect of problem solving, and then responding to what's being said by taking action. Again, the source of the problem is often feelings of not being cared about, and that their opinions don't matter. Simply acknowledging to your partner what they're trying to say is sometimes enough.

• *Put the relationship and commitment first.* Make your relationship and the love you have for your partner the most important value in a conflict. Coming down on the side of the relationship helps create a solution-based communication. If you are not working toward a solution you are not problem-solving. If you are not using compassion, understanding, respect and empathy as your solution process you are off track.

• *Apply the Golden Rule.* Do unto your mate as you would have them do unto you.

In conflict there are certain steps that if taken will lead to resolution almost every time we encounter a disagreement. After each step we need to acknowledge what was said to our partner.

Simplified Steps to Conflict Resolution

• What is the pain about? (*Source of the conflict.*)
• What are my expectations for my partner that may be unrealistic? (*Idealizations.*)
• What are realistic expectations for my partner in this conflict? (*Reality-base.*)
• What are my issues, and what are my mate's issues? (*Articulate the source of the problem.*)

- What are possible solutions? (*Solution-based discussion.*)
- What can we both do to make it better next time? (*Future-based solutions.*)
- What can I do to make it better? (*Personalize solutions.*)
- What have we learned from this? (*I.*)
- Is there a better way to talk to each other to avoid the hurt? (*Values.*)

Warning Signals

When relationships fail there are certain telltale signs that if seen early enough can turn the problem around. Here are some signs for early detection of relationship failure:

- When there is physical, emotional, or sexual abuse.
- When one or both people won't listen or own their part in a conflict.
- When there are drugs, alcohol or eating disorders that are not being addressed.
- When there are open affairs and deception.
- When there is stealing, cheating, and lying.
- When there is a loss of affection.
- When there are negative cycles and resistance to getting help.
- When there is little or no communication.
- When there is no ability to resolve conflicts.
- When there is no peace or contentment.
- When sexual relations have ceased.
- When there is no friendship.
- When there is no love.

During a couple therapy session, I was listening to a woman who felt lonely in her relationship. I asked her husband if he would turn to her and tell her how he felt. We had worked together for some time, so he was ready for this. He talked about how he was afraid that he would disappoint her and lose her love. She responded by holding his hand and telling him how much she loved him. He was surprised to find out that what she wanted was his truth and the closeness it created. He realized that his myth about being manly, keeping it all inside, and never showing his vulnerability was not working. He felt so much better when he was able to express his fears and concerns. He was very successful and highly educated, but it did him no good in his emotional world. He needed to open up and so did she. When they were able to express their deepest concerns, it connected them in a powerful way.

If a loving emotional bond is the foundation, respect is the process, and sensitivity and consideration are the rule, then our relationships will run more smoothly. Relationships do not require twenty-four hours a day processing in order to function. Once we learn to comfort and soothe the sensitive spots and ease up on our expectations, we're doing what makes love last. Nothing works all the time. Love is made from concern for the other, and the willingness to be open with our truth said with loving kindness, while providing the opportunity for our partner to do the same. Being an active participant in our relationship creates a loving place to work out issues that come up in the natural course of living.

Conflict is normal. Resolution is an art. To work through problems and differences with a loving attitude creates love. If we take the time to understand the natural complexity of a difficult interchange and then listen to the plea, the wants, and the dreams of our partner, we're in a place to love more deeply. If conflicts become a source of intimacy, then we are on the right track. It's a wonderful direction and goal to work toward with our life partner. Loving someone in a way that includes our and their imperfections will inevitably lead us to a deeply intimate attachment.

Breathing life into our relationship requires that we look at, see and understand ourselves and do the same with our mate. The dual nature of love, in that it takes two, is the essence of a romantic union. The struggle to balance our lives and to pay attention to the ebb and flow of moods, feelings, and passions is a challenge, but it's the path toward an enlightened sense of intimacy. The interwoven nature of love brings light into dark places, as we discover our true nature with those we love.

4

How Myth and Fantasy Affect Love-Making

It is very simple. It is only with the heart that one can see rightly. What is essential is invisible to the eye.

Antoine De Saint-Exupery
from The Little Prince

Is love the stuff of dreams, fantasy, and mythology, or is it something more real and tangible? Is it the product of a purposeful creation? To address the question of whether love is in our nature or truly a product of nurturing, we set our course to explore the rocky shores and sheer cliffs of myth and fantasy. How they affect the way we love is a critical component in the quest to love more deeply. Myth and fantasy offer information and challenges to the way we connect and most importantly, what gets in the way of our love-making.

There are several ways to understand how myth and fantasy function and inform us about our inner workings. They help us to understand how we create expectations that affect our ability to love. Myth and fantasy are important instruments of insight because they can enlighten us about what we want and need from each other. They allow us to enter a world of possibilities that can deepen our loving process. If we place these two different and yet related processes into their proper perspective, they can positively affect the way we love each other. Myth and fantasy offer a unique glimpse into our inner life and provide important information about what we believe, who we are, how we want to be with others, and how we want them to be with us.

Myth-Making

Myths contain both cultural and psychological information. Cultural myths originally sprang from oral tradition which was a means of passing important concepts and values on to younger generations before print was available. Myths were efforts to teach, inspire, and explain what seemed mysterious. Myths sought to explain the heavens, the tides, time, the seasons, the origin of life, how the sun crossed the sky, and why bad things happened. As man learned more and more about how things worked, the need for myths evolved into something more personal. Modern myths have focused more on explaining how and what love means as in "happily ever after," or that we have only "one true love," or the idea of an inescapable fate or destiny. Books, film, television, and music support romantic myths. Myths can overlap with fantasy or even other myths. A psychological myth might include a fantasy that if we can attain perfection then we will find that one special perfect love, or it may be overlapped by a personal myth that we will always be doomed to love the wrong person.

Personal myths about ourselves can be both improbable or completely off-kilter. We may imagine ourselves to be perfect or selfless when we're not. When we attempt to find the truth about ourselves or within our relationship, we may need to tussle with the differences between myth and reality. Myths about love abound in romantic life. The eventual goal is to understand what our myths and fantasies mean so they can be used to guide us toward a more peaceful and harmonious life.

Fantasy

Fantasy life often stems from deeply held wishes, hopes, and romantic and/or sexual desires. Fantasies may also include unrealistic or improbable mental images in response to deeply held psychological needs or thoughts of revenge and redemption. Fantasies can be negative or positive and may fill our heads throughout the day. We may see someone from across the room or walking down the street and fantasize that this person will save us, make us happy, and be the perfect sexual partner. Our fantasies may go wild and fuel our longing for liberation from loneliness or fill us with desire, hope, and excitement. Knowing what our fantasies are telling about what we want can be helpful for discovering what is missing in our lives. Fantasies function differently than myths because they occur *within* us, whereas myths can be a part of the broader culture. Fantasy is a way to look at our inner life to find out more about what has meaning to us. Interpreting fantasy is the same as interpreting a dream. Fantasies are waking dreams.

When we use fantasy to make intimate connections with others we are using it productively. Destroying myth and fantasy is not the aim, but allowing them to teach us about our internal life provides us with valuable clues about what's truly important to us. Let's look at the fantasy connected with seeing someone at a party or walking down the street. What our fantasy may be revealing is what's missing from our inner life. We may feel lonely, emotionally dead or unlovable. The person we're looking at suddenly makes us feel more alive and excited. Fantasy is then creating a better feeling about ourselves and our rather empty life. What this also reveals is the need to make our life work better. It provides vital information about our fears of actually meeting someone or being close to our mate. It may expose a sense of loss or personal numbness. For example, our fantasy about a chance meeting on an airplane and finding our true love may really be about our need to feel wanted. This is how fantasy can help us to learn about what we really need and want.

The Myth of Love

For centuries, love has remained the stuff of myth and fantasy. Love was uniquely defined by each culture according to the specific needs and mores of the time. For most of human history, romantic love was relegated to the upper classes, who were far away from the struggle to survive. Aristocrats frittered away their time pondering love's vicissitudes. It was quite fashionable in eighteenth-century France to embrace the drama of unrequited or passionate love.

By the twentieth century, romantic love had blossomed into a cultural phenomenon and the intensity of this process was heavily influenced by advertising. Romance has become big business. Diamonds, cars, clothes, even cleaning products fuel our national myth that love is somehow connected to acquiring these items. Television and film make the myth of romantic love the centerpiece of our hopes and dreams. We're besieged by a continuous barrage of romantic myths that attempt to provide solutions for our deeply felt need for love. Romantic fantasy and mythology is such a staple of modern life that it has become an end in itself. To that end, we struggle to find the one perfect love that will cure us of all our ills. That being true, we still yearn for love in all its forms, from being intimately connected to simple everyday caring. For most of us love is what makes life worth living.

Romantic Myths

A love song swells on the radio, a romantic memory floods our senses, and fantasies fill our hearts with fond memories and a renewed desire for a loved one. Romantic myths often include the notion that love completes us or makes us happy, or that we're utterly lost without it. Freud maintained that romantic longing depletes the self because all value is directed at the other to the detriment of the self. He believed that unrequited love can lead to self-loathing and suicidal thoughts. It's true that falling in love makes us happy for a period of time. Unrequited love can make us equally miserable. Even though love is important and being in a healthy relationship very valuable, we cannot always count on our loved ones to always be there for us or to continue to love us forever. In the long haul of relationships, most of us will spend upwards of seventy-five percent of our time at work or other activities that take us away from our loved ones. So, just as we crave love we must not forget to make our relationship with ourselves equally important to our overall happiness.

The more we know about our personal mythology and fantasy, the more responsive we can be to these inner promptings. For example: If we know that our fantasy of power and domination is really about feelings of powerlessness, then it helps us focus on the issue and work it through. Freeing ourselves from the control that fantasy can have over our behavior allows us to love more deeply. For love to continue throughout our lives, it's helpful to understand what role fantasy and myth play in our relationship. They ultimately provide important information that helps us evolve into more loving people.

The reality of love becomes clearer as we understand the influence that myth and fantasy can have on our inner life. The idea that love is an activity is a valuable piece of information. Then our operating principle becomes: *Love does not create itself—it must be created.* Love is not an elixir that acts on all people in the same way. For love to be emotionally healing, even redeeming, there must be a serious interest in sustaining an emotional connection.

Deeply held myths can create expectations that may have an adverse affect on the quality of our connection with our partner. If we expect love to make us happy, we will be disappointed. The myth of unconditional love without intimacy-work ultimately breaks our connection because it can't bear the weight of that mythology. In finding what's true about relationships we must search for what it means to be human. Marion Solomon writes about the importance of dependency in her book *Lean on Me.* She describes how healthy couples actively relate to each other, not dependently but "interdependently" whereby they depend on each other for help and support. This kind of teamwork both satisfies our need for connection and for sharing the load, leading to a sense that relationships can actually make life easier. Interdependency creates optimism, security and more freedom. This paves the way for independence that inevitably brings positive energy into our relationship. Herein lays the real dichotomy between mythology and reality.

The collision between myth and reality can occur in what appears to be commonly held beliefs. The Hollywood western cowboy myth that we must be the strong silent walk-alone type, or that success will make us happy still pervades American culture. John Bowlby, the father of modern attachment theory, once said, "There is no such thing as self-sufficiency, only effective or ineffective dependency." What he was describing is that, like it or not, we need one another. We suffer when we live life alone; we thrive when we feel loved. Bowlby believed that at the heart of what it means to be human is the need for social contact with others. It's the balance between creating our own happiness and making someone else happy, and receiving much needed love, support and care from our partner that fills us up inside. Myths and fantasy do not always support this idea, but they can help lead us in that direction.

Carol Gilligan, who wrote *In a Different Voice*, spoke at a conference titled "Passionate Attachments." She said, "Love is what happens when the cracks in our ideals heal up." She might just as well have said the cracks in our myths heal up. What she meant was that in every relationship, we experience breaks in our ideal of love that lead inevitably to disappointment. Love is the result of healing those breaks in our ideal (our myths) of what we believe a relationship should be. We may begin by believing in the myth of an ideal mate, but in time, we come to the realization that we're living with a human being. If we understand the difference between myth and reality we will naturally become more compassionate toward our loved ones.

Enduring love is not sustained by chemistry alone, but is fashioned from the desire to be with that one person, in reality, in truth. Expecting our myths to come true can create conflict and broken connections. When romantic myths fail us, we are left with a sense of loss, and we may feel the urge to find someone new to fit into our mythology. We will once again be disappointed. Understanding the relationship between fantasy, myth and realistic expectations is crucial to relationship happiness and adult love.

"Matchmaker, Matchmaker, Make Me a Match"

With the advent of Internet dating, we can log on at any time and read a perspective mate's profile. People express their romantic wishes and in essence put their best foot forward, describing their most acceptable traits. They present their fantasies, myths, desires, interests, and their often-idealized view of romance. There is frequently an immense difference between the presentation on a website and who shows up at coffee. For those creating a profile, their list of personal characteristics usually does not include poor self-esteem, hatred of their mothers or fathers, abandonment issues, fears of intimacy, or addictions. Although the Internet has provided a much-needed "cyber town hall," the outcome can be risky. Importantly, no matter what we read in a profile, the reality of who this person is may be much more complex. It takes time to flush out the real person from the mythology. For this reason, when considering a new relationship, it's a good idea to work in some questions. Have you ever taken time to find out who you are? What was it like growing up? What was your relationship like with your parents? How did your mother and father treat each other? Did they express love toward one another? Did you spend a lot of time alone as a child? Were there drugs, alcohol, or violence in your family? A good rule of thumb is that it takes about two years to get to know someone. Marriage is the most important decision we will ever make in life, so we must take the time to find out who this person is before taking the plunge. If we encounter some startling answers to these questions it doesn't necessarily mean we should immediately run for the hills. It should make us want to find out more, let some time go by, and see how this person reacts to new experiences before we make up our mind.

I was talking with a woman recently who was going through a difficult divorce. She couldn't understand why her husband had abandoned her so unceremoniously. She mentioned that he was the product of a divorce, never knew his father, and that his mother had deserted him. If she had thought about what circumstances he had come from and that he had never worked out his family pain, she might have saved herself some grief. He did to her what was done to him.

Another issue that warrants some attention would be whether this person reminds us of our parent. Are we really trying to complete something that was never completed, like getting someone who is distant to be close? When choosing a mate, we should always keep in mind unresolved family myths and fantasy.

Family Myths

Families customarily mythologize themselves as happy, caring, and supportive when in actuality there may be a darker interior that is not openly expressed. This darkness may be seen in depression, self-deprecating humor, petty arguments, angry outbursts, substance abuse and alcoholism.

The process of separation-individuation is a critical step in being true to ourselves. Robert Kegan in his book *In Over Our Heads*, discusses the process of distinction and separation in his chapter on healing. He considers maturity to be a set of stages from the first to the fourth order or the fully actualized self. He refers to the way families create myths with what he terms the "family religion." For Kegan the third order is the critical stage before we distinguish ourselves from our family of origin. He writes:

> The idea that leaving the third order of consciousness is akin to leaving the family religion does not mean that the move to modernity of necessity requires us to leave the family or the religion. What it requires is that we construct a new relationship to the family or the religion. Like all such metaphors sent in to aid the remaking of mind, the new spaces it can create are not necessarily separations between people but distinctions within a person, differentiations within a relationship or a faith. The prospect of leaving the family religion can foster a host of such distinctions: the distinction between having a religion and being had by one's religion; between believing as my parents believed and believing as I believe because it's how my parents believed and believing some of what my parents believed because I have come to find it is also what I believe; between finding my own way of practicing what is still a form of the family religion and leaving the faith altogether; between leaving behind some of what my parents believed and leaving behind my precious sense of connection to them. The creation of such distinctions builds a trembling bridge from the third to the fourth order of consciousness.

For most of us, the road to our separate identity can be confusing because it's so hard to know where we begin and our family leaves off. Our values and our identity, including our own brand of mythology, are the result of our entire life experience, which includes family, friendships, community, religion, and cultural education. Even though some of what we believed as children has proven not to be true, we switch back in time automatically as we touch on a previous experience that is stimulated in the present. Part of knowing ourselves better is to understand what has affected us. Our experience belongs to us; it makes up a large part of who we are. To push away or deny parts of ourselves creates separations within us. Learning to look at ourselves objectively and accepting how our history has affected us not only creates internal clarity but also helps prevent us from becoming a victim of our past. Self-criticism, self-blaming and self-destructive behavior are all manifested out of personal myths which are the product of unprocessed painful experiences.

When couples can draw distinctions between their individual form of a "family religion" and what they have come to believe as a couple, they are building a "trembling bridge" between their worlds. To distinguish how our personal, romantic, and family myths play out between each other offers hope for a new beginning and the possibility of a more profound loving experience. To leave our family mythology is to shape our own views, taking what's worthwhile from our experiences and bringing this knowledge into our relationship life.

A lasting intimacy is created by the blending of mutually formed values and shaped by an agreed-upon sense of what is satisfying to each other. Replacing fantasy and myth with reality allows us to make truly authentic connections with others. As we fully appreciate how our mythology and fantasies shape our thinking, we become more capable of seeing what's true in our relationships with others and within ourselves.

Myth and Marriage

We live in a culture of romantic concoctions, potions, and palliatives with equally high sets of expectations. For couples contemplating marriage, romantic expectations can overburden their relationship. Ted Houston, Ph.D., a professor of psychology at the University of Texas, carried out a long-term study on newly married couples. He began the PAIR project, an acronym for Processes of Adaptation in Intimate Relationships, and followed 168 couples through the first two years of marriage. He found that couples who began their relationships with a high degree of romantic mythology had a more difficult time adjusting to married life than those who started out with more pragmatic expectations of marriage. Couples with unrealistic romantic mythology were more likely to become disenchanted. Couples who did not try to maintain the romantic ideal were less conflicted. Of those in the study who got divorced, most stated that it was the loss of love and affection due to the lowering of the original romantic feelings, rather than the quality of their conflicts, that led to divorce. The natural ebb and flow of emotions for these couples was a signal that their romantic myth had failed them. Huston contends that marriage is nourished more by supporting positive feelings than by spending time trying to fix what's wrong. Couples who are desperately trying to maintain their original romantic mythology will be sorely disappointed when conflicts that are a natural part of living cannot be resolved.

Houston concludes that couples who understand that ambivalent states of love and anger can coexist in normal love relationships are more likely to stay together. He suggests that whirlwind romances fare poorly for marital success because they too easily paint an unrealistic picture of a future that often cannot be realized. Houston offers an "enduring dynamics" model for marital success, which contends that stability and predictability determine marital success more often than constant happiness and romance.

The character Dr. Iannis speaks of love to his daughter in *Corelli's Mandolin*, by Louis de Bernières:

> Love is a temporary madness. It erupts like an earthquake and then subsides. And when it subsides you have to make a decision. You have to work out whether your roots have become so entwined together that it is inconceivable that you should ever part. Because this is what love is. Love is not breathlessness, it is not excitement and it is not the promulgation of promises of eternal passion. That is just being in love, which any of us can convince ourselves we are.

Love itself is what is left over when being in love has burned away, and this is both an art and a fortunate accident. Your mother and I had it, we had roots that grew towards each other underground, and when all the pretty blossoms had fallen from our branches, we found that we were one tree and not two.

With mythic realism being hurled at us from all sides, how can we avoid the lure of romantic myth and fantasy? To find the resolution to this onslaught of misinformation about myth and fantasy we need a clear sense of reality. Reality is the true building block for love-making. The challenge is to know how to find it. The question for ourselves is how invested are we in the idea of love as a salvation or a cure for what ails us? Knowing how our attitudes are shaped by culture and experience helps us to see more clearly into what we are about. If we grasp the nature of our lives and what drives our world, we won't be disappointed when our love relationship has its own sets of difficulties. The search for what is real is an active, ongoing process and is the product of thought and dialogue with others we trust.

Realistic Expectations for Love

- Our feelings ebb and flow.
- Relationships require perseverance.
- Ambivalence is expected.
- Conflict is inevitable.
- Differences are desirable.
- Trust is earned.
- Kindness is crucial.
- Empathy is required.
- Humor helps.
- Sometimes saying nothing works best.
- Don't try to change your mate.
- Acceptance creates peace.

Reality Check

Moving from fantasy to reality is a pivotal process. To help understand this we will take a quick look at what reality looks like over time. Daniel Wile tells us that all couples move from romance to disappointment to alienation. He notes that couples cannot do anything to avoid disappointment but can overcome states of alienation by talking about them, thereby decreasing the distance that alienation creates. He believes that alienation is a natural part of all love relations. The ability to release negative feelings through discussion brings about the return to a more intimate state. He also categorizes couples into three main relationship conflict patterns:

- **Mutual Withdrawal:** when couples respond to disappointment by mutually withdrawing.
- **Mutual Accusation:** when couples blame each other.
- **Demanding-Withdrawal:** when one partner makes demands and the other withdraws.

Relationship dynamics involve what Wile terms the "pursuer" and "distancer" type of interactions, where one member of the relationship is pursuing while the other is more passive or distant. Wile believes that couples may exhibit any one of the three patterns depending on what mood state they're in. One week a couple may be mutually blaming, then more withdrawn, and the next week they may take turns blaming and withdrawing, or there may be a more stable pattern of blame and withdrawal as a conflict style.

Couples will often try to avoid conflict because it can be so counterproductive. But if couples can learn how to make conflict productive, they will be more willing to face it and thereby create a deeper intimacy. When conflict styles involve screaming, name-calling, hitting below the belt, and angry demands, both people will surely avoid confrontation. When couples break up, it's often because they can't organize a problem and find a mutually satisfying solution.

Imagine an interaction that goes something like this:

Him: What's wrong?

Her: What you said hurt my feelings.

Him: What did I say?

Her: You said that I care more about my friends than you, and that is not true.

Him: I know I said that, and it was how I felt at the time. I think sometimes that you treat them better than you treat me.

Her: You know, now that you say that, I think you're right. You know my mother was always on the phone with her girlfriends, and I felt that she didn't care about me. I guess I'm treating you the same way. I think that I'm so concerned with how my girlfriends feel about me that I forget about you. I take you for granted. We can't forget how much we mean to each other; we have to always remember how much we love each other. I think I have to work on my need for approval from others and consider where that is coming from. I can see that my need for approval would make you feel that I care more about my friends than I do about you.

This dialogue may seem too perfect and to some extent it is, but in a healthy relationship a conversation like this can actually be that good. We notice first that neither one was defensive. The open quality of the encounter helped to move it along to a positive conclusion. We can easily see what worked here. Their willingness to listen, see the other side of things, and then respond with a positive statement dissolved a possible conflict.

Understanding how our feelings change from our romantic beginnings requires that couples know something about what causes those changes to occur. In the normal course of events, feelings toward our mate flow in and out organically, riding the crest of constantly shifting tides of emotion. Most people experience a full range of emotions and moods from love to annoyance, from comfort to anger, from commitment to ambivalence, from joy to displeasure, from passion to jealousy. When couples accept that romantic feelings continually ebb and flow, they are more firmly planted in reality.

Relationships that survive do so because the people in them understand how to make grief important, pain productive, and conflict a learning experience. Intimacy is made out of good communication, the acceptance of differences, perseverance, the capacity for tenderness, the ability to bear ambivalence, and striving toward peaceful problem solving. When couples allow for pathos, turmoil, and confusion while maintaining their sense of balance, they will survive, even prosper in the straits and narrows of the changing landscape of intimacy.

Redemption

Redemption is an act of forgiveness even absolution for behaviors or thoughts past and present that we have never made peace with. It registers as a relief from feelings of loss, shame, or guilt which have been eradicated through a redemptive act. Redemption can also be based on something like a fantasy that being loved by a certain someone will heal a bad feeling about ourselves. It's about reclaiming something that was lost. Another form of redemption might be to humiliate someone as retaliation for being abused as a child. Or if we suffered from not feeling wanted, then being wanted would feel redemptive. It's an innate need to want redemption. Someone who felt unwanted as a child may attempt to be desired by as many others as possible. A man may obsessively work to be wealthy so he can be redeemed from feeling valueless. A woman who grew up poor and felt ashamed of her poverty may believe in the myth that marrying a rich man will redeem her. The fantasy that someone will make us whole, lovable, and adequate is a natural urge. Romantic myths tell us that love will redeem us from loneliness. Redemptive fantasies of perfection, financial success, or being desired are all attempts at changing something bad into something good. The question is, does it work?

Seeking love as redemption for our personal misery can't work because it's based on a myth. Love can offer only temporary relief from inner misery. The myth that someone can save us from ourselves is a powerful source of hope. Realistically our partner can only be intermittently available and at times will be unable to meet our needs. The difficulty with redemptive myths and fantasies is that they alter reality. Understanding the reality of what relationships can provide allows us to look into the truth about what we really want.

The origin of redemptive fantasies can be traced back to our earliest experiences. They originate from our coping strategies for getting along with others. Many children grow into adulthood never realizing that they felt alone. Children can confuse duty or admiration for love, while inwardly hurting and not knowing why. Expressing love, admiration, or duty that is devoid of emotional content is still isolating and painful. Our effort to find the perfect "Mr. or Ms. Right" is so often a fantasy wish to heal our deep sense of loneliness and an attempt to create a sense of self-worth.

Once we've found our ideal person and get married, feelings that have lain dormant for years may break open, and with them depression, anxiety and defensiveness. If our mate disappoints or fails to measure up to some aspect of our early coping mythology, it may stimulate the original sad and angry feelings. Then we may turn on our mate and blame them for our unhappiness which creates conflict. This is how a redemptive fantasy can be destructive.

Red Hot Romance

When Helen and Jim first came in for couple therapy, she was hopeless and he was worn out. It was immediately clear on meeting this young couple that they did not understand what was causing their arguments and were unable to identify what was wrong. Helen had thought she was marrying her ideal man and consequently was deeply disappointed in her husband. Jim thought when he married Helen that she was totally accepting of him and was completely surprised that she was critical and unhappy with him. They had lost hope that their difficulties could be resolved.

Helen described a painful childhood. An autocratic father forced her to be obedient while her mother's fragile emotional states turned her into a caretaker. She was physically abused by her father, and her mother's alcoholism and subsequent depression prevented her from coming to her daughter's aid. Helen became a mother-substitute for her sisters. To distract herself from her misery, she would dream that someday her prince would come to save her from her feelings of being unlovable.

Helen met and soon married Jim, who seemed to be the savior she had always dreamed of. They had lived far apart during their courtship, allowing them to create naive fantasies that acted as a shield against seeing the deeper issues. Helen was now thirty-five years old and felt that if she didn't grab this guy fast she might not get another chance at having a family. So she pushed hard to become exactly what Jim wanted her to be so they could speed along toward marriage.

Jim's parents were college professors who placed a tremendous value on education and scholarly performance. Although Jim was able to achieve academically, he felt his parents paid almost no attention to who he was inside. He feared that the approval he got from them was based solely on his ability to perform in school. Jim's mother was a perfectionist and withdrew when he made mistakes. As Jim matured, he dreamed of a woman who would love him for who he really was. He wanted to be accepted for himself, not because of what he could achieve. Without realizing it, Jim married his mother.

During their courtship, Jim and Helen were active socially. Consequently, they were rarely alone. They didn't often speak of their inner life or how they had suffered. When they were first married, they continued to be gregarious, traveling with friends and engaging in social activities. Soon into their marriage, they decided to have a child.

Prior to the birth of their first child, Helen was still acting like a mother-substitute to Jim, but secret resentments were simmering just below the surface. As Jim became more successful as a stockbroker, they decided Helen should stay home and raise their daughter, but soon difficulties began to arise. Helen wanted Jim to be handy around the house but he procrastinated because he was too insecure and scared that she would be critical of him. Helen's perfectionism reminded him of his mother and made him feel inadequate, so he shut down. Jim would experience anxiety attacks when asked to do something as simple as changing a light bulb. Helen would upbraid him for his passivity and saw his difficulty with household work as proof that he didn't love her. She would explode with rage at what she felt was his laziness. She described him in unflattering terms like, "He's a slug." This would cause Jim to become sullen or move to a superior position as if he had better things to do than change light bulbs. Jim and Helen were powerless to resolve their conflicts because they didn't know how to express their emotional complaints.

Jim was a procrastinator, and not very attentive, but otherwise a loving husband and devoted father. Helen wanted Jim to be her ideal man. Her knight would rise early and shoulder part of the load with their daughter by getting her ready for school. Then he would be off to work with a spring in his step. Her ideal man would listen, complete projects on his own and be an overall ultra-responsible, sensitive, caring, and proactive new-age kind of guy. Based on this idealized version of a husband, she was despondent about what seemed to her a horrible choice. Jim had tried everything but could not make Helen happy. When Jim didn't meet Helen's Prince Charming fantasy, she became critical, contemptuous, blaming, and depressed. When Jim did not do what Helen expected of him, she would take it personally. She would say: "If he really loved me, he would help me and keep his promises." When Jim tried to defend himself, she would lash out at him. He bitterly and righteously complained, "I'm damned if I do, and I'm damned if I don't." They were at an impasse.

Interestingly, both Helen and Jim were different in their private sessions than in their couple sessions. In their individual sessions they were able to see what was going on psychologically in a way that they were unable to do when they were together. I developed an idea about how to treat the problem. I felt that because they had the ability to be sensitive and flexible with me, if they could translate that same process into their relationship then we might just be able to begin a resolution process. As Helen and Jim started to feel even more comfortable in their intimacy with me, with some urging they began to open up to each other. What we discovered was that neither of them had fully internalized a commitment to their marriage. They secretly believed that divorce was a way out. They were always secretly preparing to leave. When they finally decided they wanted to make a full commitment to their marriage, they could accept that it was up to them to make it better. So Helen and Jim began to communicate their fears and concerns. Because they had been so emotionally withdrawn, when they did actually communicate their concerns there was immediate improvement.

The expectations of redemptive fantasy and perfection were the culprits here. Helen and Jim tried to live their fantasy ideal and it just didn't fit with reality. This romantic fantasy operated as a mask that served to hide their fear and loneliness. *When they finally opened up, out came two angry children who were terrified to be seen for who they thought they really were.* It was difficult for them to understand how their personal issues were being expressed in their relationship. Helen's romantic fantasies were a means of defending against her fear of abandonment. They offered her a sense of possibility and hope. When she couldn't be perfect it opened the door to her internalized anger, causing her to be righteous and vengeful. This made Jim feel inadequate and he retaliated by passive withdrawal, which angered Helen to no end.

When Jim and Helen understood that their poor self-esteem affected the way they related to each other, they realized what needed to be done first. After some positive work on self-esteem they began to more clearly express their wishes, desires, and needs. The practice of actively communicating their feelings worked well for them. As of this writing Helen and Jim are still together and have another child. They learned that if one of them is having a problem, it doesn't mean there is a loss of love.

A Piece of the Puzzle

The example of Helen and Jim teaches us something about commitment. Helen held onto the option of leaving so she wouldn't have to come face-to-face with her pain and low self-esteem. To deepen her commitment to her relationship she had to look at her personal issues. Her dedication to the marriage hardened her resolve to face her personal demons and understand how they affected her relationship with Jim. Statistics show that unmarried couples who first live together have a much lower success rate than married couples committed to staying together. The deeper the commitment, the harder people work. They have a stake in making their relationship run more smoothly. When Helen and Jim finally made a commitment to making their marriage work, instead of looking for the exit door, they worked to find solutions because it was in both of their best interests. The idea of commitment however, is not a thing in and of itself. Commitment involves the day-to-day activity of making love work. It does not mean that simply being committed is the answer, because there are no pat answers. If we decide to be honest, with an open mind, we will have a better chance at a lasting relationship. If we believe that there is something better just over the horizon, it weakens our commitment.

Gertrude Stein is famous for saying, "There is no there there." So, there is no there to get to; it's right in front of us. The grass turns out not to be greener on the other side. And as Bukaroo Bonzai once said, "Everywhere you go, there you are." Our issues will follow us everywhere we go, and to think that some one thing will save us from ourselves is unrealistic. Relationship happiness is an active process and requires external support and internal acceptance. Loving each other, finding interesting work, developing our personal life, and finding the joy in gratitude and forgiveness are the essentials of happiness. So it may not be in our nature to always be happy, but it is the pursuit of happiness that can create it. To bring a whole host of activities, relationships, and exciting personal adventures into our life is making happiness from the inside out.

To see and understand the logic of our myths and fantasies offers up not only our own wishes and truth but the path to a better life. Myths and fantasy provide a true glimpse into the interior of our soul. With this knowledge we can forge a loving future.

5

How Love-Making Leads To Making Love

Sex contains all,
Bodies, Souls, meanings, proofs, purities, delicacies, results, promulgations,
Songs, commands, health, pride, the maternal mystery, the seminal milk,
All hopes, benefactions, bestowals
All the passions, loves, beauties, delights of the earth,
All the governments, judges, gods, follow'd persons of the earth,
These are contain'd in sex, as parts of itself, and justifications of itself.

Walt Whitman
From *Leaves of Grass*

Sexual Healing

In my experience with couples, sex is like a snapshot of the relationship as a whole. Because it's such a powerful experience, it taps into the core of relationship health and connection. For couples who feel close, supported, safe, and loved, sex tends to be a regular and pleasurable activity. When people feel unsafe, unloved, and not secure, sex is usually problematic. Couples who come to therapy with sexual issues usually need to look deeper into the quality of their connection. Generally, if they're not sharing intimacy, it's indicative of a break in their emotional bond. Other factors that influence sexual dysfunction can be related to trauma, stress, inhibition, drugs, alcohol, performance anxiety, early sexual abuse, rigid religious upbringing, self-esteem issues, or physical illnesses.

Sexual dysfunction may indicate unresolved personal and relationship conflicts. People who are obsessive-compulsive, rigid, angry, demanding, or lack the ability to be empathic or tender with their mate will most likely experience sexual difficulty. Angry, controlling, and sadistic partners may find outlets for these issues in their sexual conduct. Sex works best when couples agree on what they want from their sex life. It is so unique and individual that psychologists generally don't standardize sexuality. Sex is different for everyone, and there is no one-size-fits-all when it comes to preference, frequency, or activities. It may range from acting out dramatic sex scenes to the mundane, from highly romantic and affectionate to perfunctory. There are no hard and fast rules for engaging in sexuality (no pun intended). Each couple must find their own way. Curiosity and communication about pleasure creates excitement during sexual play. Not everyone craves extremes in their sexual encounters, so tastes can range from intense to calm or sweet depending on the individuals involved. The point is that both partners agree with the type of sexual activity that is occurring.

Sexual Agendas

Sexual desire may be the product of fantasy, or it can be exploited as a means of control. For example, we may want sex to validate our self-worth or to control someone so they will do what we want, or as an outlet for anger. Adding these extra components to an encounter can cause the other person to feel that our desire is not really about them. The resulting experience can be a "turn-off" because we're made to feel like an object in the other person's emotional struggles. Alternatively, the enjoyment of sex is personal and specific to each person. What brings pleasure to a couple can be whatever they want it to be. The important part of a sexual encounter is for couples to agree on what they want and make it a mutually satisfying experience.

There is rarely an exact match in desire for sex between partners. At any given time, one person may want more or less sex than the other. Difficulty arises when there is pressure for sex when the other one is not interested or is turned off. Sexual patterns change throughout life and are subject to shifts in desire based on things like stress, illness, depression, monthly cycles, birth of children, and aging. Couples who survive the ups and downs of sexuality do so because they communicate with each other about their interests and desire.

When couples are goal-oriented and march straight to orgasm, it can cease to be about desire for the other person but instead become desire for the effect that sex has. Sexual intention may contain a multitude of issues like expressing anger, pressure to make the partner orgasm because we need approval, to succeed or to possess them. If we detect that sex has become harmful, this must be addressed or we risk the possibility that it will interfere with future sexual encounters. Flushing out the rationale for a sexual difficulty no matter how hard it may be is the first step. If one person always determines when and where sex will occur this may prove to be a problem. The general rule is: for sex to be satisfying, couples need to work out a way to balance the desires of both people. Sex works best when both people feel connected emotionally, psychologically, and spiritually. Otherwise, sex may become just mutual masturbation and the ability to create a loving connection may be lost.

Generally speaking, men want to have sex to feel close; while women want to feel close to have sex. Simone De Beauvoir points out in her groundbreaking book *The Second Sex*, that men and women experience sex differently because women are being entered and men are entering. So while men feel closer because they're entering, the woman desires closeness first to allow a man to enter her body. In American culture, it's acceptable for women to show affection toward each other, but men are not typically very affectionate with anyone outside their love relationship. Sex for most men is their main resource for feeling close, vulnerable, and how they give and receive affection. This same difference would include male gay sex where there is often an emphasis on sexuality, not necessarily intimacy, while with gay women there is generally more attention paid to affection and sensuality.

Sexual problems are often related to unresolved anger and bitterness. When a woman tells me that she does not want to have sex with her husband or lover, it's typically because she feels a loss of respect and connection with her mate. When sex diminishes or dies, it's usually because of the constancy of angry exchanges, negative words and actions, not communicating feelings, or an emotional stalemate.

The Desire Factor

Desire is the X factor in relationships. Desire emanates from some primordial internal place that is as much mystery as it is known. If we factor in symmetry, body type, height, weight, hair color, skin color, or how our partner smells, walks, talks, and moves, we see that there are some consistent patterns that emerge. Scientists have studied American sex idols and have come up with a mathematical formula that predicts whether someone will be considered sexually desirable or not. It is based on the relationship between head size, waist size compared to the rest of the body, and the balance between head, torso, and legs. For many men, weight, breast size, leg length, hair and skin color will determine their level of desire. For most women, the desire factor is not necessarily limited to physical attributes but is more often related to traits like reliability, trust, sense of humor, strength of character, morality, or security. Our source of desire or lack of it may also have something to do with a parent, either because we have unresolved issues with them or because we identified with or loved them.

When we find ourselves looking for the right match, what are we looking for? Social scientists have been studying this for years. In 1952 Erving Goffman came up with a matching hypothesis which stated that people tended to choose partners who were similar in degree of good looks. T.H Huston in 1976 postulated that people choose a match based on looks because they want to avoid rejection. L. Brown stated in 1986 that people choose according to what they feel they have to offer the other person. These factors being present may create attraction, but what is it that maintains it? Again we must turn to love-making and our ability to continue to be desired based on how we behave.

The question is, how do couples in a long-term relationship continue to have an active sex life? For those who are working in high-pressure jobs with children, finding a time and place that is conducive to sex does not often present itself. Making a time for intimacy is one of the best ways to make it happen on a regular basis. Otherwise it might not. In this way couples are being proactive about their sex life and insuring that it will occur on a more regular basis.

The more couples communicate about their sexual interests and desires, the more satisfying it can be. Problems with inhibition or attitudes toward sex need to be discussed and worked through. Creating desire through affection, humor, sensuality, or fantasy will encourage a more satisfying sexual relationship. Talking about what turns each person on and creating the space for sex are the basic ingredients for continued desire.

Sex is the most sensitive of human experiences. For this reason how we talk about sex to our partner is very important for continued contact. Masters and Johnson in their cutting edge work *On Sex and Human Loving* made an important point about sexuality when they said make "no" sound like "yes." Something like, "I know that you love to put your tongue in my ear, but I get so turned on when you kiss my neck." In this way she made a no statement sound like a yes statement.

Some Questions to Ask

- Where do you like to be touched?
- What's your fantasy about great sex?
- What makes you anxious about sex?
- Show me how you achieve orgasm?
- Do you feel pressure to achieve orgasm?
- What turns you on the most?
- What do you like most about foreplay?

What's Good Sex? It is...

- Playful.
- Accepting.
- Easy-going, relaxed.
- Communicative.
- Sensual.

- Non-goal oriented.
- Can be about what feels good.
- No pressure.

Some Ideas About Sex

You make the limits: You can define sex any way you want it to be. There are no "shoulds" in sex. If something is not working, then you need to find out why or let it go. Talk through anxieties and fears, and then take the pressure off. Obviously, a soothing, patient approach works best. People are very particular about their sexual interests. If couples like having sex in exactly the same way every time, then so be it. The best approach is to find a way that works for both of you.

Do not take anger to bed unless you like it that way: If you find that you are holding back, or losing desire, you may be angry. If there is tension in your relationship, you will feel it sexually. Your past experience with sex may be interfering with your present situation. If you were abused somewhere along the line in your life or are being abused in your present relationship it will affect you sexually.

Orgasms: If women have questions about orgasms, consult *The Hite Report* by Shere Hite. It's an excellent book on female orgasm. For sex to be satisfying for a woman, she may want to express her desire for orgasm through helping her partner to assist her in achieving it. Hite discusses the idea that women orgasm differently. To understand that difference requires communication and experimentation.

Erections: Erectile dysfunction or the anxiety about it can cause sexual inhibition. For more comfort with sex there are a few things to consider:

- Erections are not the only way to experience pleasurable sex.

- If the penis does not respond, there may be a very good reason.
- Many men feel they must react with an erection if any woman wants them.
- Perhaps she is just not attractive to you.
- Perhaps you are not comfortable with her.
- She may be altering her behavior so you won't lose your erection and it's a turn off.
- Try getting and losing an erection with your partner. Begin intercourse and then stop, take a break, allow yourself to lose your erection, and then get it back.
- Losing an erection is due to the shifting of blood from your penis to your heart, especially when you feel anxious.
- You may come to find out that you are nervous or scared of something about your partner. The best course at that point would be to talk about your fears to help you relax.
- Take your clothes off and then just hold each other. Affection can be satisfying.
- Erectile dysfunction can also be a response to a medical problem such as alcoholism, drug abuse, underactive thyroid, hypertension, prostate problems, or diabetes.

Spiritual Sex

Spirituality has become of more and more interest in American culture. This upsurge in spiritual pursuits includes Zen Buddhism, Kabbalah, Tantric exercises, and spiritual sexuality.

Tantric sex is a disciplined practice that attempts to join love and sex. Margot Anand has written a book titled *The Art of Sexual Ecstasy* as a resource guide for couples wanting to work toward a spiritual sexual connection. She writes:

When sex is just an unconscious, mechanical urge in you, it's wrong. Remember, sex is not wrong; the mechanicalness of it's wrong. If you can bring some light of intelligence into your sexuality, that light will transform it. It won't be sexuality any more ... it will be something totally different, so different that you don't have a word for it. In the East we have a word for it, Tantra. In the West you don't have a word for it. When sex becomes joined together, is yoked with intelligence, a totally new energy is created ... that energy is called Tantra.

Fantasyland

Sexual fantasy as distinguished from our earlier discussion of myth and fantasy is similar yet distinct from other aspects of our fantasy life. Sexual fantasy can specifically relate to sexual encounters or can take on other aspects of our personality, like power or pain. Sexual fantasies can be positive or negative. They can play a role within a relationship or be completely separate. They can either add to our relationship or create distress. They are by nature not reality. We are the director, writer, lighting tech, and cinematographer in our sexual fantasy life. Sexual fantasies inform us about our deepest desires, whatever they might entail. They may relate to punishment and submission, or may be devoted to romance and redemption. In this sense, fantasy can be bound up with more profound desires. Sexual fantasies contain important information about our inner world. A negative fantasy can contain frightening or abusive visions. Positive fantasy may portray a romantic scene like making love to our beloved on a moonlit beach somewhere in paradise. This leads us to ask, what can we realistically expect from our sexual fantasies? If we think of sexual fantasies as dreams and see them as what Freud would term "The royal road to the unconscious," they offer a window into the soul of our desires. By understanding fantasies we may be able to uncover what we need from others that may give us great satisfaction. If we fantasize about submissive or dominant partners, it may be a compensation for feeling too responsible or too submissive in our daily lives. Couples can refer to fantasy as a means of learning something about with whom, what, and where our sexual satisfaction really lies. Sexual fantasies, if expressed appropriately, can contribute to the intensity of sexual life.

It is not necessary to act out or share our fantasies. Sometimes allowing for fantasy is enough. Fantasies can get our thinking oriented toward intimacy so that having sex with a partner can be more intense and satisfying. Fantasies can be especially helpful for older couples who have been married for many years and for whom orgasms are more difficult to achieve.

Fantasies reveal our yearnings. Even though fantasies contain our desires, wishes, and needs, they are most valuable when they're used as guideposts and not rules for life. The ability to have fun with fantasy is a key element to making the most of our sex life. Our ability to discuss fantasies openly with our partner leads the way to greater understanding and connecting with each other.

John's Secret

John grew up in a home with extremely passive and emotionally fragile parents. He was seldom able to express his intense feelings or anger toward them, and when he did they withdrew and/or fell apart. His repressed anger was so great that, at a very early age, to pacify himself he turned to masturbatory fantasy that contained images of inflicting pain. He had to "be nice" and passively accommodate his parents to gain acceptance and love. Once he sexualized his anger, he found a perfect outlet. His parents had no control over his fantasies, so he began a rich, inner sexual life of pain and dominance.

His sadistic wishes toward his parents developed into sexual fantasies in which he could express his aggression and anger in relative safety. By the time he reached adulthood he had completely sexualized his rage toward his parents. When he began to be intimate with women, his sadistic dominating urges emerged. Once he married, he turned his sexuality toward bondage, dominance and sado-masochism. In this way, he was able to experience the parts of himself that he could not access or vent in daily life.

His sexuality will more than likely not change much, but knowing what his fantasies mean will enable him to discuss them with his wife and use this information to improve their sex life. His understanding about how his aggression became sexual allows him to use this energy in his work and social life for more effective relationships in the world. His insights into the origins of his sexual preferences freed his wife up to share her intimate fantasies and as a result they have made changes to accommodate her.

Harry and Sally

When Harry met Sally they were in their late forties. Harry was previously married to his high school sweetheart who had become pregnant at seventeen. In those days it was unacceptable to have an abortion or to have a child out of wedlock, so they married. It was a mismatch from the start, and after many years of trying, they divorced.

Harry grew up in a home that was emotionally distant. His father rarely showed Harry affection or interest. His mother was dedicated to his father and his younger sister. Harry mystified his parents. He was a dreamer and loved to draw and make things. He became an architect. He tried all his life to gain his father's approval but never received it.

Sally was raised by nannies and maids because her divorced mother was very successful and often away on business. Her father disappeared early in her life and died when she was quite young. Her mother was controlling and strict. Sally could not express her anger toward her mother without very serious consequences. Sally was outwardly happy and carefree but angry and pensive inwardly. She became a successful surgeon, but due to rigorous academic demands her social life failed to develop normally.

Both Harry and Sally had been single for many years when a friend fixed them up. They were quickly enthralled with each other. Sally saw Harry's artistic nature as the unfulfilled part of herself, and Harry enjoyed how much Sally loved his work. They moved in together early into their relationship.

After about a year, their sex life began to wane. Sally felt a lessening of her sexual desire for Harry, who constantly pressed for sex. Sally responded by withdrawing. Harry became angry and sullen. He reacted to the lack of sex as if Sally were his disapproving father. He felt rejected and angry when Sally tried to talk to him about her lack of interest. She felt resentful that he wanted sex for his self-esteem needs and not because he desired her. Harry was angry because he felt rejected, and Sally was hurting because she felt controlled.

When Harry and Sally arrived at my office, they were both very frustrated. Harry complained that Sally was controlling, and she countered with the belief that he only wanted sex to satisfy his own needs and not her. In my private talks with Harry, a set of insights began to emerge. His low self-esteem contributed greatly to his need for sexual validation. It made him feel wanted. Sex had taken on another meaning.

Sally came in by herself and during our session she realized how Harry's demands made her feel. Once she could see that she was experiencing her mother all over again in Harry, she decided to be more generous with Harry's self-esteem needs. She experimented with Harry and tried to be accepting of his desire for sex. She saw that sex was her gift of love to him. As Harry grappled with his self-esteem needs, he understood how much his desire for Sally had to do with his need for validation.

He realized that he didn't need to make sex a battleground because it affected their intimacy. They mutually came to see how much of their personal issues were involved in their sex life. Harry and Sally developed a pattern of intimacy that worked for them. These days Sally asks Harry about his desire, and they play with fantasy during the week and make time for sex on the weekend.

Sex, like all adult processes, is integrated and embedded in couple interactions.

Understanding what role sexuality plays in our relationship helps us gain insight into who we are together. Sex is a wonderful outlet for the expression of love. Sex can be a barometer for the health of the relationship. If sex is a guest, then we can be a good host by making time to be together and using things like fantasy to increase excitement and pleasure.

6

Separation And Reparation

Sometimes our light goes out but is blown into flame by an encounter with another human being. Each of us owes the deepest thanks to those who have rekindled this inner light.

Albert Schweitzer

In all relationships, breaks in the emotional connection will occur either from alienation stemming from our busy lives or from empathic failures. Lapses of empathy are part-and-parcel of everyday life. *The important issue is how we resolve them, not that we experience them.* Empathic breakdowns are based on emotional disconnects from within or between each other. Breaks in empathy are a normal part of life, but the key is in knowing how to repair them. Anger, criticism, emotional withdrawal and blame are common causes of empathic failure. If we're paying attention, we can feel the break when it happens. How we heal emotional disconnects has a lot to do with our ability to tune in to our own internal promptings but also with tuning in to our partner.

If we never learned how to repair empathic breaks growing up then we will have difficulty with our present relationship. We use what we have learned and if we don't understand what we're doing then we're likely to blame our partner for it. If our only method for solving empathic breaks is to become punishing or withdraw, we may erode our emotional connection. Once we know how and why we disconnect from our mate, we can find out how to re-connect when it happens. This critical skill can only widen the possibilities for creating an emotional bond.

Anger may also function as a method of holding on emotionally in the midst of a break. Anger and/or rage are such powerful connections that many couples will unknowingly move toward those states because they don't know another way to connect. While doing couple therapy, I discovered that some couples would not forfeit their anger or rage. No matter what I tried, they seemed to go back to anger. Finally it occurred to me that they needed the anger to maintain their connection. They seemed relieved when I encouraged them to continue to do what they were doing because the pain of isolation was too great. Once couples can grasp the intention of their anger, they are free to discover new paradigms for connection based more on loving kindness rather than anger and withdrawal.

Some Thoughts on Healing Breaks

- Make sure you have a good understanding of your partner's feelings.
- Ask yourself if what you are doing will maintain the connection or break it.
- Think about what needs to be said to repair the break.
- Do you need to apologize?
- Being loving and kind allows you to be heard.
- What are your feelings telling you about what you want?
- Acknowledge (saying back what you heard) your partner even if you don't agree.
- Try out different resolutions to find what's comfortable for both of you.
- If you're not working toward a resolution you are on the wrong track.

Reparation

Repairing emotional breaks is an essential ingredient in love-making. Reparation comes in many forms, from talking about what's hurting us, to writing a letter, to keeping a journal, to simply making time to discuss whatever it is that needs attention. If couples are apprehensive because of abandonment terror or fear of humiliation, they will keep their distance. In this way anger becomes a way to be connected while maintaining a safe distance.

Our psychological wiring and sense of well-being is based on living for thousands of years in tightly bound tribal clans. We naturally seek connection and feel lonely when we don't belong to a group or to a person. One idea that seems to come up while working with patients is the limitation of even two-parent families. It becomes starkly evident from all our social conflict and the rise of gangs, cliques, celebrity, and sports fanaticism that we're missing our village roots. The loss of our tribal or community connections has in many ways created a void in our need to belong. Anthropologists tell us of primitive societies that stay cohesive by referring to all men as father and all women as mother. I'm immediately struck by the notion that children in these environments have a wide array of choices of adults who can meet their needs for comforting and connection. These children rarely fall through the cracks, as many children do in one or two-parent working or dysfunctional families. In smaller family units, children may not always have access to a parent and as a result become isolated, which may make them feel worth less and/or unlovable. At the heart of self-blame and self-criticism is a lonely child. Most couple conflicts are based on the need for connection. Within each family, couples may experience various defensive styles that lead each one away from the hurt and lonely child within.

Conflict Styles to Avoid

- **Turning the argument around:** A very common defense is to turn the argument back onto the other person by saying "You do that, too." Turning the argument around is a non-productive communication style and needs to be pointed out so the conversation can continue about what each one is feeling and what needs attention within the relationship.

- **Hitting below the belt:** Learn how to avoid the tender and painful emotional areas in your mate. Even though it's tempting to retaliate by hitting someone below the belt, it should be avoided at all costs. There are words that can be said that can never be taken back, forgotten, or repaired. Like crystal, once broken, you may try to repair it, but the cracks and sensitivity that breaks in trust create will remain. If your mate confides in you about an experience that is very sensitive and you bring it up in an argument to use against them, you are hitting below the belt.

- **Denial:** Denying that you did anything to hurt the other person creates more conflict and contempt. If your partner is telling you that you hurt them, chances are you did something to upset them. To deny it only adds fuel to the fire. The best solution is to stop and validate their feelings first. "I see that I did something to offend you. I'm sorry; I did not intend to harm you."

- **Bringing up the past:** Another dysfunctional style is to bring up a list of injustices that have been saved up and then are dumped out on the other person during an argument. These injustices serve as a distraction from the point and are meant to direct the blame back onto the other person.

- **Setting fires:** Some people set fires to distract from the real issue. For example, if your mate brings up your stinginess during a discussion about his or her overspending, this is setting a fire to distract from the original subject. Breaking down into hysteria, storming out, slamming doors, hitting walls, drinking excessively, screaming, or bringing up some other problem during a discussion about something else are all distractions.

- **Denying the truth:** There are those who will lie to save their own skin in an argument. At the bottom of all this is the fear of feeling bad about oneself or defending against loss. Lying in an argument only makes it worse. If the lie comes out, then trust is broken and that may be difficult to resolve.

- **Bringing others into an argument:** "Even your mother thinks I'm right." When your partner feels that you won't listen and they get frustrated enough, they will bring others into the fray as a desperate attempt to get through. If you want it to stop, then start listening and see what happens next.

Resolution

The healthier people are emotionally, the better the relationship will be. The responsibility for good connections lies within both people. We all wish that someone could take our pain away or give us a magic potion to make our problems disappear. There is no secret potion, but if there were one, it would be our willingness to look at, listen to, and understand what our partner is trying to tell us, and then to try to respond accordingly. If we function well in our relationship, it will be because we're willing to reflect and learn about ourselves from our interactions with our mate. To shine a light on all the dark places is one of the basics for creating intimacy. Respecting our mutually sensitive spots and learning how to soothe them enables us to turn toward our partner and not away. If we make an effort to resolve our relationship discord, we will be actively working through our own issues as well. Letting our partner know that we deeply understand them is a very powerful instrument in the loving process.

Making a Vision Statement

A vision statement is a footpath that guides us in our quest for an evolving, loving process. A vision statement might be about something like unfolding, harmony, or mindfulness. We make vision statements because they help us define what's important. These statements can be present in all aspects of our relationship. Vision statements can be spiritual, religious, philosophical, or practical. They set the style and tone for decisions and direction. A vision statement is only one way to create a relationship ethic. Other means of ethical and moral identity are finding areas of mutual interest like volunteering, philanthropy, creative activities, or extended family. A vision statement is an active process. It creates discussion and strengthens purpose and connection. Couples need things they can do together. Vision statements can be continually changing and transforming, making them an ongoing source of interest and connection. The clearer we are about our relationship values, ethics, and beliefs, the better able we are at creating the harmony and empathy that forms the basis of our safety and security.

Some Vision Statements

- Unfolding love.
- Harmony in our relationship.
- Ecstasy as a goal.
- Loving kindness in the way we treat each other.
- Creativity in the way we live.
- Tenderness toward each other.
- Circle of life as our commitment.
- Joyousness as our life goal.
- Humility in all things.
- Charity toward others and each other.

Making a Resolution Statement

After we have ended a fight and know more about what the problem is and what the relationship goals are, it's time to make a resolution statement. For example, "I promise to listen and do something about being more attentive if you will help me by understanding when I have to work late." This statement allows for the ideas and concerns of each person to be voiced and agreed upon. This is a good way to keep the agreements in place to avoid the same problems in the future. The important point here is to do what we say we will do. If our partner can see that we're trying to do those things we have promised, they will feel touched and more in love with us. If both people make an effort to do the things that they agree on in resolution statements, there will be longer periods of harmony. Remember though, it's much easier to *know* what to do than to *do* it. Old habits die a long and slow death.

Some Ideas for Harmony

• **Teamwork:** If you see a full wastebasket, it won't kill you to empty it. If you take off your clothes, it only takes a minute to hang them up. If you see that your mate is tired and give them a hand, they will love you more for it. These small things can have a large effect on feeling loved and cared about. Other examples of teamwork are: working out a budget that both of you can live with, making improvements that you both feel make your home better, finding a television show that both of you like, or reading together.

• **Love frames:** George Bach was one of the first psychologists to talk about discord in relationships. He offered a means of avoiding conflict and creating more love with a concept called "love frames." For example, "I feel the most loved by you when you buy me flowers," or "I feel the most loved by you if you rub my back or want to be intimate with me." The other side of that becomes what each person does to show their love, such as: "Whenever I want to show you how much I love you, I wash your car," or "When I'm feeling especially loving, I want to cook you a great dinner."

• **If you want something, ask!** So often people simply expect the other person to "know" what to do without ever being asked. It's like sex; no one knows exactly what will bring you to orgasm but you. If you don't tell the other person, they may not know. The rule should be that if you cannot ask, you cannot get angry with your mate when you don't get what you want.

• **Acting on agreements:** Whatever you agree to as a result of repairing an emotional break, if you follow through, you will create positive feelings.

• **Negotiate and compromise:** When you can't agree, take a step back and look at some alternatives that might make both of you feel good. Negotiation and compromise make up a large part of all decision-making for couples. Learning to find a comfortable place for both of you is the hallmark of relationship health.

Big Expectations, Big Disappointments

For perfectionists, expectations are about the right way to behave and something that others are just supposed to know. They deem that their expectations are the way people should live life. They are astounded and angry when their expectations are not met. The perfectionist in love often believes that one should be romantic and selfless all the time. When this doesn't happen they think that their lover has failed them. Expectations are a natural response to our environment. But most of us don't feel compelled to meet all of them. We see our expectations as a guide and a goal to work toward. But there are those whose need to be perfect is extended to others. In a mature relationship this can become a major source of contention. Let us for a moment examine our expectations.

Here are what unrealistic expectations sound like:

If you really loved me you would make love to me every night.

You should always know what I want.

You should always know what to do to make me happy.

Obviously, the other side of expectation is disappointment. Expectations are idealized or fantasy versions of real life. Disappointment is our reaction to the difference between our fantasy and reality. When we can't meet these expectations, we feel like a failure. When we attempt to do everything we can to meet our partner's expectations but can't fulfill them, we will stop trying. If, on the other hand, we have realistic expectations, then what our mate actually does is greeted with happy surprise. *The critical point is to know what realistic expectations are.* To find realistic expectations we need to understand what we want and need from each other. In this way we can learn what we can expect from our relationship and what may be too much or not enough.

Expectations are often built on unmet personal needs. The less able we are to meet our own needs, the more we will expect from others. But this doesn't mean that we must meet all of our own personal needs or that we can't depend on others. For expectations to be realistic, they must be founded in reality. Can my mate give me some of their time right now, or are they too busy? Why do I need my husband to tell me he loves me so often? The more we fantasize about how others "should" be in order to soothe our personal insecurities, the more we will expect of them and the more disappointed we will feel.

Let's take for example the expectation that others should be on time. If we're always on time, then we tend to expect others to do the same. We get angry when others aren't punctual. We feel justified in our anger at our mate or friend. After all, they were being disrespectful. As we begin to look into the origins of time issues, we see that not everyone was raised the same way. Some households just don't run on time, and the children in those homes may never have learned to be on time. As we look deeper into ourselves we may find that our anxiety about lateness is connected to fears of abandonment and insignificance.

Learning to manage expectations through understanding and empathy toward others can only have a positive effect on our relationships. Recognizing that we're making others responsible for our anxiety about time helps us to develop more realistic expectations to work through our deepest fears. Importantly, we must ask ourselves what's more important, our righteous indignation or our relationship?

The task of working out our anger and anxiety is the key to keeping expectations healthy. If our mate is the only resource for anxiety reduction because we can't work it out on our own, we will create an expectation that they will always be available to help us when we need them. This is not a realistic expectation. No one is that available. It creates a natural state of disappointment and resentment on both sides. If we can't work out our own fears, anxieties, and expectations, then we will look for help. We can't afford the fallout from this behavior. It will erode our connection. The resolution is obvious; we need to take care of our own anxiety and relieve our mate from being solely responsible for neutralizing it.

No two people can be connected all the time, so it is only reasonable to assume that there are natural breaks that occur. Repairing those inevitable breaks lies in our ability to understand what's needed to create peace of mind. Love-making is about our unique dance that is based on self-knowledge and listening to the music of our distinctive way of relating.

Alienation is unavoidable. If we place this knowledge firmly within our realistic expectations we will not overreact when we experience the inevitable loss of connection. Learning to consciously and thoughtfully create connections based on an intrinsic grasp of what's real allows us the freedom to experiment with different and unique relationship ideas. To play with and venture into new worlds with each other gives rise to innovation and rebirth, all of which brings us from distance to intimacy and from anger to joy.

7

How To Turn Complaining
Into Love-Making

*Loving someone is knowing the song in their heart
and singing it to them whenever it begins to fade...*

Unknown

In all loving relationships complaints will naturally arise as an inevitable part of living closely with another person. If we respond to complaints as unwelcome or intrusive we're likely to create even more problems. Working out complaints can help make our relationship run more smoothly. *Complaints are not to be confused with criticism.* There is a difference between the two. A complaint sounds something like, "I know you care about me but you rarely tell me that you do." A criticism might sound something like: "You're such a jerk; you would never say anything nice to me, it's always all about you." Criticism is a personal attack, whereas complaints can open up a discussion about how to make it better. Criticism is often a response to hurt feelings and is intended to hurt back. Complaints are communications that express needs and wants. Airing complaints is necessary for relationship health, good communication, and harmony. Expressing complaints clears the decks emotionally so they don't become criticism or create distance. If complaints are also expressed with tender loving care it further creates a more positive atmosphere. Criticism pushes people away and creates more hurt and anger.

Complaints can take many forms. One person may complain about being neater than the other, or about them forgetting to put the cap on the toothpaste. People believe differently, or were raised with different values, or have differing tastes and aesthetics. They may think differently about how they should spend money or even how to live life. These differences present a ripe environment for complaining. If complaints are not expressed or effectively resolved, they can deteriorate into resentments that may eventually lead to emotional distress or deadness. Resolving complaints is a catalyst for change and greater contentment.

Common Complaints

- Not enough quality time.
- Not enough intimacy.
- Not enough affection.
- Not enough expression of love and concern.
- Not enough consideration and respect.
- Not enough empathy and compassion.
- Not enough concern for the concerns of the other person.
- Not being reliable.
- Not expressing appreciation.

Jack and Fern

"We don't have a marriage," Jack opined. It was clear that he felt frustrated. He complained that Fern was always too tired for sex. He wanted her to be there for him like she was when they were dating. Early in their marriage, Fern became pregnant, and soon after went back to school to finish her bachelor's degree. He was afraid that if he told her how hurt and rejected he really felt that she would call him a baby. For Jack to express the source of his complaints would mean he might hear that she didn't care about what was important to him. Deep down, Jack believed he was unlovable. He criticized Fern for being overweight, and that she didn't cook for him. Although his criticism of her may have had some merit, he didn't realize how much anger was coming from his feeling that he really wasn't worth it. Jack's anger and criticism of Fern turned her off. Her stonewalling caused him to feel even more frustrated which then escalated the conflict. They were at an impasse. After I had several sessions with Jack alone, he began to understand the depth of his concerns and that his deepest fears were unfounded. During our next session he was able to ask for and receive reassurance from Fern. When she found out how he really felt, she was more than willing to tell him that she loved him and would not leave him.

If couples draw on complaints as a resource for understanding each other better and in a deeper way, those very complaints become a way to create greater intimacy. When couples are successful at resolving complaints by responding to them with understanding and compassion, they're actively creating security and loving feelings. To understand and acknowledge the validity of a complaint is to be empathic. Empathy is at the heart of all emotional connections. If empathy is a leap of compassion, then to take that leap is to hear and express complaints in a way that is non-critical. The most powerful thing we can do during an argument is to acknowledge what our partner is saying to us. Acknowledgment is a way of relating intimately because it requires that we listen with compassion. It involves using insight to demonstrate that we understand what was said, and in this process we emotionally connect with our mate. When we feel acknowledged we feel attached.

During a conversation in therapy, a woman was complaining that every time she and her fiancé started to discuss marriage he withdrew emotionally. She suddenly realized that he acted out his fears instead of talking about them. He would arrive late for dinner, was non-communicative, and would forget to follow through on agreements. When she got angry he would react by stomping out or hanging up on her. Then he would pull away citing her anger as the cause. She would consequently rant at him about his inconsiderate and disrespectful behavior. He would justify his actions and then leave. Because she had felt abandoned as a child, his passivity and withdrawal stimulated her outrage. He was afraid of losing his freedom and of being trapped in a relationship that he couldn't get out of. When they did get together, they had terrible fights about his behavior.

These two didn't have a clue as to what they were doing. He was afraid, and she reacted to his passive behavior by becoming angry. They had lots of complaints. They needed to see that their behavior was a way of *acting out* their fears instead of discussing them. When she could tell him how much she needed him without the anger, he was more sympathetic. They worked out a way for him to feel he had some autonomy and still could make plans so that she could count on him.

Negative Cycles

- When one person stonewalls and the other ramps up with anger.
- When either one blames the other for their own bad behavior.
- When either or both people use withdrawal to express anger or to punish.
- When there is mutual withdrawal, mutual blame, and mutual criticism.

Everyone's Talking, But Is Anyone Listening?

With most couple therapy books, media psychologists, and various pundits, a great deal of attention is paid to the importance of communication. John Gottman discusses communication in his book *The Seven Principles For Making Marriage Work*. Interestingly, he believes that talking everything out is not always the cure for what ails relationships. He asserts that some couples talk very little and still seem to be happy. It's logical to assume that easygoing couples have less antagonism and are more compatible and well-matched than others. It doesn't seem likely however, that intimacy is truly possible without communicating feelings, needs, and wants on a regular basis. It's often just not important to discuss normal everyday irritations because they are not really about anything.

If our partner continually does something that is offensive or hurtful to us, we have to discuss it if we don't want to become resentful. Some relationship issues are persistent and rarely ever go away completely. Therefore, there is little need to discuss them. The key is to know what's important and what will pass. If our partner repeatedly uses sarcasm to express his or her feelings, then it must be addressed if we find it offensive. The trick is to know the difference between what can be worked through together and what is just a part of the way life is.

Does Compromise Mean We Are Both Unhappy?

To compromise is to find a place where both parties can agree—a mutual comfort zone. When we compromise, we have to be willing to give up *some* of what we want, but not *all* of what we want. When couples are too busy fighting about who's right, or trying to win the argument, or are attempting to change the other person, it renders them incapable of compromising.

Once in a couple's therapy session my patient Steve mentioned that he and his wife Amy were having difficulty agreeing as to when he should come home after being with his guy friends. He wanted to be with them to decompress from work stress. Early in his relationship with Amy, he had gone to a prostitute after one of his nights out, so after that, whenever he was late she would become frightened and anxious. She was not sure what her husband was going to do, and her own history was fraught with abandonment issues. Steve was controlled as a child and felt alone much of the time. As a teenager when he was alone he would masturbate, and over time this fantasy life evolved into going to prostitutes. He didn't understand why he was continuing this behavior. His acting out sexually was creating an enormous amount of pain for Amy and he knew it. As a consequence their issues around compromise were much more complex than what was on the surface. They needed to look deeper into their history and fears before they could work out an agreement.

We talked about Amy's issues, and Steve really listened because he did love and care for her. She was able to be more considerate of his difficulties once she understood how they came about. He worked out his issues regarding his need to decompress in ways that were more positive, and decided to build a workshop where he could make furniture as an alternative to going out with the guys. Finally, Steve was able to value the importance of his commitment to his marriage and was willing to compromise. He realized that he had a responsibility to care for Amy's feelings. She was greatly relieved and promised him that as long as he would keep in touch with her she would not be angry at him for being late.

By working out a compromise that acknowledged each other's feelings, they were able to connect on a much deeper level. As they understood what they were experiencing, they created a more intimate bond. As they mastered the way to process their disagreements they created a positive dialogue that went something like this: "You're telling me that you feel terrified when I stay out late and don't call you. I will never do that again." And in response: "I will try to understand your need to decompress as long as I know that you care about how I feel."

Transformational Listening

The core component of active listening is acknowledgement. One could also describe active listening as active empathy. The ability to acknowledge re-establishes our emotional connection when it has been lost. Once we have listened and responded, the next step is to turn to our partner and ask how we can make it better. *It's striking how couples will fight and scream at each other about what they are not getting, never realizing that the very act of screaming will deny them the opportunity of getting it.* If we use anger to get our point across, we can expect anger in return. If we express our point of view with compassion, respect, and understanding, we're much more likely to get a positive response. As I am writing this I'm struck by how obvious this idea really is. So why do couples have such a difficult time understanding what seems to be so simple? What may be true is that fear, low self-esteem, and childhood grief create enough chaos internally to cause massive shifts of energy and create formidable defenses against what feels to the person like a possible rejection or humiliation. Therefore, we react with anger, not fully realizing that we have slammed the door shut on the possibility of getting what it is that we want. Only with great care can we unearth earlier events in our lives that shape the way we interact with others in the present.

Susan Johnson writes in her book *The Practice of Focused Couple Therapy: Creating Connection*;

> Couples must move from alienation to emotional engagement, from vigilant defense and self-protection to openness and risk taking, from a passive helplessness in the face of the inexorable dance of the relationship to a sense of being able to actively create that dance, from desperate blaming of the other to a sense of how each partner makes it difficult for the other to be responsive and caring, from a focus on the other's flaws to the discovery of one's own fear and longings, but most of all, from isolation to connectedness." The essence of what Susan Johnson describes is that we must be willing to risk opening our hearts and expressing our deepest fears and longings, in an effort to create a connection with our mate. Otherwise, relationship distance will ultimately claim us. Johnson aptly points out that emotion is the music of the couple dance.

Relationship harmony and love are in many ways created from repairing broken connections. Resolving complaints is one way to repair a severed emotional bond. It's difficult to change a lifetime of emotional reactive patterns and then see clearly what our personal responsibilities are when we're hearing complaints from our partner. It takes time and patience to create new pathways for emotional connection. When couples learn to express complaints without criticism and hear them without becoming defensive, they are actively strengthening their connection.

Complaints are often dimensional and include different facets of our emotional life. The important consideration is *why* do we do what we do, and why do we do it the *way* we do? How does it serve us? Is it possible that the reason we're not listening to our mate is because we're angry, or feel unloved, unimportant, or invisible, or all of the above? Criticism, defenses, anger, and resistance to compromise may be indicative of broader and deeper issues. If we're willing to look into the complexity of our responses to complaints and the reasons for them, we may learn something new about ourselves and our relationship. What are we getting out of complaining or being complained about? Is it that we are upping the ante by screaming at them so they have to listen to us, or is it that we're trying to protect ourselves from failing in their eyes, or being rejected? *If we allow ourselves to look inward and speak the truth we see there, then touch our partner's vulnerability with our own, we are actively harvesting the energy that can create love.*

In a letter to his brother, the poet John Keats used the term "negative capability." He was referring to a coping skill that enables us to manage the negative aspects of life. Couples often fantasize that love is easy and that one should be happy. Then when negative events occur, we want a crutch to hold us up and there isn't one. Instead of yearning for this idealized life, we must learn to see differences and difficulty as a natural part of life and not insist on one single rule or force of will. This is a hard lesson.

One way to think about marriage is to consider it from the standpoint of one who is living between two countries with different cultures, desires, states of mind, wants, and needs. Then, we can think of ourselves as a good-will ambassador. By using diplomacy we can create peace and harmony with our neighboring country. If the countries are to get along, they must use proper protocol, kind greetings, good manners, cordiality, and consideration. Considering marriage like this is a good way to think about what it means to create a loving environment. So often couples unwittingly behave as if they have a free pass to say or do whatever comes to mind. If we believe that love is earned, we will be much more likely to think about what we say and do. Being civil, diplomatic, and thoughtful will go a long way toward being heard, accepted, and respected.

Love-making includes giving compliments and expressing complaints: "Thank you for taking the time to make a lovely dinner," or "When you borrow my car, I would appreciate it if you could make sure you check the gas on the way home." People tend to be quick with criticism and late with compliments. There is a reason. Saying positive things about our mate makes us feel vulnerable, and negative comments make us feel powerful. Human beings are wired to protect and defend against pain or humiliation. We fear being hurt or being thrown away. The truth is there is no completely safe way to love.

Creating Safety Requires...

- Feeling that our partner is looking out for us.
- Knowing where our partner's wounds are and learning how to avoid stimulating them.
- Asking for and receiving comfort when we need it.
- Knowing what makes us feel loved and what we do when we love.
- Feeling valued and respected.
- Not letting complaints build up.
- Creating a healthy interdependence.

We're all afraid to love deeply and to put our heart in the hands of another. Our ability to count on someone, to feel like they've got our back, is critical to making a safe place to love. Taking time to work through complaints, getting to know our mate, and understanding what makes them hurt, feel loved and cared for, will allow our love to emerge from behind the safe but isolating walls that protect us.

Dr. Howard Marksman, professor of psychology at the Center for Marital and Family Studies at the University of Denver, conducted a study of more than twenty marriages that lasted twenty-five years or more. He found that relationships in which couples experienced the highest levels of satisfaction were those that had developed joint problem-solving abilities. Dr. Marksman calls "constructive arguing" one of the best predictors of marital success. He discovered that couple's *differences* were not the all-important indicators of marital success but rather *how couples handled their differences*. How people go about resolving differences is a predictor of how intimate a couple can be. When we think about how we want to handle those differences it makes sense to be prepared. Are you merely looking to win? If you want peace, love and harmony, then you must remember to add those elements to your communication style.

What Promotes Relationship Success?

• Listening with compassion, respect, and consideration.
• Empathically tuning-in to what your partner is thinking and feeling.
• Listening to what's said and acknowledging first before responding.
• Sticking to the principle of the complaint and not dwelling on the particulars.
• Working toward comfortable compromises.
• Making room for differences.

When couples see how their defenses work and how their own fears and insecurities are affecting each other, they will be able to reconstruct their conversation. Insight can be daunting, but continuing negative interactions that are actually about old baggage is counterproductive. Developing practical insight keeps our intentions clear and facilitates the resolution of conflicts. This kind of enlightenment broadly means the acquisition of compassion as an intention. In that sense, enlightenment is moving toward the light of positive thinking so that positive behavior will follow. Knowing who our partner is, coupled with our willingness to talk about what's bothering us will help us to actively create both inner tranquility and a loving environment.

Are we willing to learn how to live well with others and take the time to find out how our mate truly sees us? How many of us have learned from our mistakes? If we want our partner or our children to love us, what must we do? What we must do is to become the kind of person who deserves to be loved. Getting there is the hard part. If couples do take the time to look into what makes them angry, selfish, mean-spirited or sad, then all that understanding and internal knowledge can be implemented with each other all the time. The most important relationship we will ever have is with ourselves.

Hidden Agendas

Joan's father had abandoned his family when she was just three years old. Her mother was so distraught and emotionally fragile that it became Joan's job to keep her from falling apart. She became mother's little helper, the dutiful daughter who dared not express her needs or anger for fear of overwhelming her mother.

Harry's parents were emotionally distant. They didn't express feelings directly; they just engaged in heated political arguments. In this way they could indirectly vent their deeper emotional pain. They had great difficulty expressing tenderness. Instead they were generous with money and gifts.

Joan wanted her husband to be more attentive and emotionally open. From her early experience with her fragile mother, Joan couldn't allow herself to have needs of her own. She became depressed and didn't understand why. She couldn't express her need for comforting because when she tried, Harry would respond by giving her a lecture about being more self-sufficient. He would berate her for not helping him enough, but when she did, he criticized her efforts. She felt there was no way to win. Joan would end up sitting alone in a darkened room, utterly depressed and hopeless. They would not speak for days. Eventually, the mood would pass, but they were deadlocked in a distant emotional state that neither knew how to change.

Therapy began amidst sadness, frustration, and loneliness. However, what did become glowingly apparent was their commitment to being married. They simply could not communicate their feelings and needs or be comforted by each other. In therapy Harry discovered what made him angry. He believed that Joan didn't respect him. Everything he said to her came out angry because he was so hurt. He also began to realize that feeling disrespected made him feel she didn't love him. What was true is that he didn't feel adequate to her love. He was taking it out on her. She wanted to know how she could succeed with him. Harry talked about feeling disrespected and unlovable once he understood where it came from. Once he could grasp that his feelings about himself were impacting how he saw Joan, he began to talk more freely about what he needed from her. He asked her if she loved him, and she was touched. She could then tell him how much she loved him.

Joan learned how to ask for help and to make plans to be together. As Harry learned how to talk about his feelings and needs for love and concern, they were able to solve the issues that were causing their negative arguments. They developed a new process where they could use their internal feeling life whether positive or negative, as a means of maintaining an emotional connection.

Claude Levi-Strauss, in his seminal work *Tristes Tropiques*, set the tone for social anthropology through studying the indigenous people of Sao Paulo, Brazil. While studying tribal culture, Levi-Strauss found that he could not apply the classical notions of anthropological research. The culture he was studying didn't fall into any predictable pattern. He discovered that the only way to create an accurate cultural model was to develop the model from the culture itself rather than from any preconceived notions about what the tribal culture should be. He classified the people from within the culture as opposed to a superimposed structure. He illustrated his point by describing how the tribe members tattooed themselves. When he copied the tattoo on paper, it bore little relation to what it looked like when it was applied to the three dimensional person. The same is true of relationships. We must derive meaning from the way the relationship is and not from what we think it's supposed to be or from what we have learned from our family. We must construct a new meaning, something that creates a relationship model from the needs and wants of each person within a unique relationship.

Our lives are chock full of stress. How we understand and work out the complexities of everyday life will determine how happy we will be. Our ability to find creative coping strategies for natural dissention and changes in life is a critical step toward relationship health. Stress is normal; distress is not. How we handle our worry, anxiety, and fear will affect the levels of contentment in our relationship. Anxiety can create strife, and because we each experience it differently, we cannot always communicate with our partner what our anxiety is telling us about what we want. Again, we need to assess the situation to determine if it's appropriate at that moment to ask for comforting or if our partner is simply unable to help us at that time.

Some Life Stresses That Can Cause Conflict

• Spouse becoming ill.

• Money issues.

• Children being born into the family or leaving home.

• A family member who becomes ill or injured.

• Loss of job, or career change.

• Aging or death of a family member.

• A spiritual or philosophical change of one or both people.

• Increased workload.

• Spouse returning to the work force.

The Source of Anxiety and Fear

Anxiety and fear can affect the way couples communicate and react to each other. When anxiety and fear are present they can create tension which in turn causes antagonism. Anger is more easily stimulated when these emotional conditions are present. Our ability to work through anxieties can play an important role in lowering tension between each other. When couples recognize that anxiety and fear are present, they can work together to comfort and soothe the tension so it does not erupt into anger.

Michelle Craske, Ph.D. of the Anxiety Clinic at U.C.L.A describes anxiety as the "misapprehension of a future event." Anxiety is linked to the feeling of dread that something bad will happen. Anxiety feels like an eight-hundred pound gorilla just rounding the next corner. We are anxious about loss, being hurt, dying, getting sick, abandonment or doing something wrong. Verbalizing concerns in an atmosphere of acceptance helps calm us. Discussing anxious negative fantasies can help us develop a more accurate sense of reality. Anxiety is future-thinking and to some extent past-thinking. We fear bad things happening or we ruminate over our past experiences as to whether we felt accepted or not. In any event, we are not functioning in the moment. Couples can work their anxieties through by talking about the unreality of the anxiety and then finding the reality together. This can both alleviate anxiety and bring them closer. Not talking about anxiety may create emotional distance and make anxiety more intense, and therefore cause more stress.

One source of difficulty for couples is not understanding how to process anxiety and fear, or not being aware of how their anger and fear may appear in their anxiety and depression. Couple conflicts are often based on anxieties about abandonment or the loss of love. Couples will incessantly argue about unrelated issues and are frequently unaware of how anxiety and fear are affecting them. As couples learn how to alleviate anxiety and allay their partner's fears, they will not only be closer to the source of their conflicts, but actively exploring possibilities for creating love. We all witness our world differently. All we really know, and not always so clearly, is our own experience. If we take our differences into account, we can work out solutions to our fears and anxieties. If we take the time to learn from our mate about what's important to them and what makes each of us uncomfortable in different situations, we will inevitably be more able to soothe and be soothed. If couples have conversations that include their fears, they will feel acknowledged and supported. The more we are able to work through our fears and anxieties, the better we will feel.

Good Solutions Involve

- **Describing what you are feeling:** "I'm afraid to love you because you could leave me." When you are angry, anxious, or fearful, take time to consider what's causing it. What need, frustration, hurt, guilt, or fear is being stimulated and is triggering anger or defensiveness? Think about what's happening with your partner. Try checking out what you think you understand. Your ability to make a distinction between your own mythology and reality is a key to working through anxieties and the stress that comes with it.

- **Defining the anxiety:** First, make sure you understand what's bothering both of you and then describe what you are anxious about. Each of you then can talk about your fears and anxieties. Take turns working out the reality in the here and now while understanding that the anxieties and fears feel real to both of you. Working out money, time, health, and family issues helps to ease them.

- **Creating calmness:** Expressing fears and anxieties not only creates serenity but also simplifies them. Calming statements sound something like: "The reality is no matter what we are afraid of we will work it out and we will be O.K." "Whatever it is, we're capable of finding the right solution if we put our heads together." "As long as we have each other we will find our way."

- **Remembering what's important:** Stick to core values and beliefs that help to give you strength during difficult times. Strong values are very effective anxiety relief systems. The more you are able to nurture each other during times of anxiety and stress, the better you will be at calming them. Talking about how much you value your relationship can help ease anxiety.

Pick Your Battles

Healthy couples usually know what to let go and what must be worked through. When considering a disagreement we must ask ourselves, how often does this come up, and is this disagreement important enough to spend the time required to resolve it? Is it something that will never change, no matter how much we put into working it out? If something our mate does continually bothers us and we find ourselves resenting and turning away from our mate, it's time to talk. If a behavior is annoying because we're anxious, stressed, or in a bad mood, probably the best course would be to chill out and let it go.

The theme of this chapter is about changing common complaints into more love and intimacy. If we actively listen and make an effort to find out about what needs are being expressed, our mate will more often respond with compassion and concern. If we can use our basic desire for love and harmony as a means of turning complaints into calming statements and discord into compassionate discussion, we are creating a source of intimacy. Efforts to soothe each other's fears and anxieties will lead us toward solutions to our most vexing relationship issues. The factors that make relationships work involve resolving fears and anxieties and expressing our deepest feelings, desires, and wishes, all operating in concert with each other.

Our inner and outer processes can be likened to instruments in an orchestra. When we are in harmony we make beautiful music, and when we aren't there is dissonance. When our inner melody is playing out loud to our partner we will find harmony. Rhapsody is often used to describe love. Our ability to listen to the sonorous sounds of our partner and the better we know how to play our internal instruments, the more we will be making enchanting music together.

8

Does Monogamy Matter?

No adultery is bloodless.

Natalie Guinzberg

A commercial features a young couple dining *al fresco*. She is pretty and he is handsome. He spies two very cute young women walking past him. He surreptitiously checks them out in the reflection of his cell phone. His girlfriend is watching this and sends him an admonishing text message with a sly grin, to which he answers, "What?" What this little vignette implies is that men have a roving eye and women have to accept it. So, how can we consider monogamy in a sexually provocative society? Is it possible to stay monogamous for a lifetime, especially for those who marry young? Most animals and certainly all primate species with the exclusion of some *homo sapiens* are promiscuous. Statistically, men are more likely to be unfaithful than women. With this in mind we will travel this well-worn territory to find some new answers to the age old question, why monogamy?

Why do people have affairs? We watch the news dumbfounded to see one of the most beautiful and accomplished women in the world, distraught and divorcing because her husband had an affair with the nanny. We scratch our heads in dismay. Are men prewired to be promiscuous? Or is it a personal or relationship problem that is being expressed in an affair? Some people seem to need sexual attraction to feel the transformational power of feeling wanted. There are men who need to conquer women to feel powerful. The intensity of a new sexual experience can add excitement for those who feel bored. The most common reasons for infidelity are loneliness, lack of appreciation or feeling unloved. Love affairs begin with commiseration and often end with a multitude of painful imperatives. Affairs begin in a flurry of passion with some even evolving into a lasting relationship. But in most instances the pain that was created in the initial moral lapse continues in the new relationship. As affairs create new beginnings, the original moral failures can return with a vengeance. When we don't do the work to find out what has caused the original failure, we are doomed to repeat it.

Monogamy is a cultural ideal in the United States. It's standard for straight and gay committed relationships. It is not practiced throughout all cultures. Plural marriage is found all over the world but is illegal in America. During the sixties and seventies "open marriage" was tried as an experiment with couples looking to bring the sexual revolution into the organization of marriage. It failed because the culture of monogamy was too strong. Many couples broke up or discontinued the practice.

So, how do we integrate sexuality, excitement, and monogamy into our relationship while viewing interest in extramarital or re-lationship infidelity as a sign of relationship stress? Sexuality is the most powerful human interaction. It's an intense yet fragile emotional system within a relationship. Sexuality and desire are affected negatively by anger, contempt, disrespect, fear, distance, and passivity. To have an ongoing sexually monogamous relationship, couples need to understand what their partner needs from them and then work to provide it. If we feel the need to act on our attraction for someone we should look both at what may be going wrong with our connection as well as what may be off-kilter internally. When sex works, it's because couples open up about their fears, feelings and concerns. When couples engage in an erotic dance that involves exploration, fantasy and playfulness, they are creating sexual excitement.

Sex doesn't work when couples make it a battleground for other relationship issues. For example, a woman may not want to have sex because she doesn't feel close to her partner. This creates stress within the relationship. If the couple doesn't resolve this issue, a battle may ensue, where one partner feels misunderstood and the other sexually frustrated. Sex is the meeting ground between men's emotions and their desire. For many men sex may be the only place they feel comfortable expressing tenderness, affection, and their need for connection. Right or wrong, when either partner declines to have regular sex, they are effectively opening the door for the possibility of affairs.

Sexuality is what distinguishes marriage or a romantic relationship from friendship. Over time passion tends to diminish, but it can continue if couples make time for it and clear the path toward it. Couples who seem to have the most active sex lives over time are those who make it a priority and work together to make it exciting.

Esther Perel explains in *Mating in Captivity* that men are all too often "over-feminized" into being passive and holding in their aggressive sexual urges. She emphasizes that aggression is a positive attribute for sexual passion, and too much talk can disturb the intricacy of independence that is a source of sexual mystery and therefore sexual interest. To her, couples need to focus more on eroticism and sensuality rather than on pressuring the other for goal-directed and performance-based sexuality.

Sex Basics

- Make your own rules.
- Experiment with sensuality and erotic play.
- Work out anger, resentment, and alienation that get in the way of good sex.
- Be open about what you want.
- Make time to be spontaneous.
- Talk about your fantasies, likes and dislikes.
- Allow for non-judgmental discussions about sex.
- No pressure, no blame.

It's remarkably human to look at attractive people. There is no harm in looking. When we feel the need to act on it, then we are creating the potential for pain. If we decide to go outside our relationship to resolve a problem that is within ourselves or with our partner we will add a bunch of pain to the mix.

Sex Slows or Stops When:

- It becomes a battleground.
- Either person is critical.
- It becomes a power struggle.
- Both of you feel alienated.
- There are no other expressions of love.
- There is a depression in the relationship.
- One of you withholds sex.
- There is a loss of respect.
- There are lies and betrayal.

Another reason for infidelity is when there was not enough attraction in the first place. People get together and marry for all kinds of reasons, and many times they choose someone they feel is a good person even though there is a weak sexual attraction. When we choose someone for reasons other than sexual attraction as an element of being together, we may lose all attraction over time. At this point one or both people may reach out to others for solace.

This is not to say that sexual attraction can't grow over time. There are occasions where even arranged marriages can become romantic. Love can bloom if people treat each other with loving kindness and compassion, but relationships of convenience can also be lonely and painful and are a ripe environment for being vulnerable to others.

The Girl Can't Help It

Megan and Carlos were high-school sweethearts. She was the very popular cheerleader, and he was a cool senior with a car. It was a match made in high school. He seemed so much older then. He was the kind of rebel type that the girls went wild over. For Carlos, Megan was his dream girl. She was popular, and he was the guy from the other side of the tracks. Soon after graduation they married. Megan wanted out of her house and away from her controlling father and depressed mother. Carlos wanted Megan because he believed her sophistication and family wealth and status would make him whole. What they did not know was that they were going from the family frying pan into their relationship fire. Megan and Carlos had almost no understanding of the complex issues that drove them toward each other and inevitable disaster.

Carlos was a "latchkey kid" until his parents arrived home at around 7:00 p.m. He was the youngest of three children, and after his parents divorced he fell through the cracks. His mother worked two jobs and was continually exhausted and frazzled. His father was a meager provider and was frequently unavailable. When he did show up, he bullied and criticized Carlos. As a result, Carlos felt deeply inadequate. He couldn't express his anger toward his father because he would have been punished for it, so he internalized it, but inside he was boiling.

Megan's unhappy childhood was laced with frequent emotional withdrawals and punishments. She was never allowed to express her anger. To protect her fragile connection to her parents, she learned to hold her feelings in and be the "little princess" her father wanted. But on the inside Megan was seething with anger. As a teenager she delighted in sneaking out during the night to have sex with Carlos, knowing that her parents would disapprove and go crazy if they knew. One of the reasons she selected Carlos as a husband was to make her father angry, to get back at him. Her anger at her father fueled her attraction to Carlos. She was unaware of how her anger at her parents made him attractive to her and how this same scenario would play itself out in their marriage. Soon after they graduated Megan and Carlos eloped.

Carlos fantasized that Megan's love for him would make him feel acceptable. Inevitably her love was not enough, and he became reactive and critical. He began to treat her like his father had treated him. He defended against his own sense of inadequacy by expecting Megan to be perfect. When she failed in his eyes, he bullied her, making her do menial tasks over and over. He believed that Megan's main responsibility in life was to take care of him, over and above their children. He thought that it was his right as a man to make all the decisions and be in complete control of her. His inadequacy forged his righteousness along with a set of rules for her behavior that supported his arrogance. He blamed the world for his personal failures. He was cheated out of his childhood and Megan was going to make up for it. He believed that Megan was his property. He convinced himself that this was his right as her husband. His criticism, power struggles, and controlling behavior were the product of his unconscious desire to weaken her so that she would not leave him. Instead of feeling weak and helpless, Carlos transformed himself into being bad and powerful.

When they initially came for therapy, Megan angrily complained about the endless criticism heaped upon her by Carlos. "Carlos is angry and critical all the time," she protested. "Everything I say starts a fight." He seemed eternally dissatisfied. No matter how much she tried, he found new things to complain about. Interestingly, Megan had become a successful executive working her way up in a major corporation, while Carlos couldn't hold a job. His wife's successes made him feel even more inadequate, which drove him to become even more demanding.

After years of suppressing her anger and rage toward Carlos, Megan rebelled. She began having extramarital affairs with his friends and others, and left a trail a mile wide for him to find. Megan was not aware of the magnitude of her rage.

Before coming to couple therapy, Megan had seen a therapist who recommended that she tell Carlos of her affairs to establish an honest relationship. When she confessed her infidelity, his worst suspicions were confirmed and it blew the top off his smoldering rage. For Carlos, this was a bitter irony. He had married Megan to be loved in a way he had never been loved, and instead it had become a nightmare of rejection and humiliation. He was profoundly wounded by Megan's infidelity. His internal defenses concocted a rage-filled cocktail that transformed him into a righteous victim. From the victim position he tortured her to no end. Megan tried talking to him, but whenever she did, he became furious to the point of violence. It became clear that Megan was simply enacting the same method of expressing anger that she had as a teenager. She didn't realize that her anger toward Carlos drove her to retaliate by having affairs. Once she discovered what she was doing it was too late, the proverbial cat was out of the bag.

Once Carlos discovered the affairs his fragile emotional system broke down and his rage overcame him. Megan and Carlos' marriage broke up because the wounds of betrayal were too dark for him to understand or accept. Not only was his trust broken, but it also confirmed something that he could not acknowledge to himself, that he felt he was inferior as a man. He had to go on the defensive because the confirmation that he was inadequate was too painful. Megan and Carlos did not have the emotional resources and personal knowledge to endure the struggle that ensued. Carlos pursued her in a relentless and nasty custody battle and subsequent divorce.

Ironically, as soon as Megan realized she was acting out her rage through sexual indiscretion, she immediately stopped having affairs and began confronting Carlos with her negative feelings. Had she done that during the marriage they might have been able to avoid the pain and suffering that followed.

Carlos' shame was now so buried that he could not connect his inadequate and weak feelings to how humiliated he felt. He remains righteous, arrogant, and bitter, blaming Megan for his fate in life. Megan went on to marry again and is now able to confront her new husband with her complaints. She no longer expects to be perfect.

A Cautionary Note

Telling the truth is essential to relationship trust but it must always be tempered with concern for the feelings of others and the perception that certain truths will indeed inflict enormous pain. Confessing indiscretions is always painful. We must be sure that this admission serves the purpose of bringing the relationship into a better place and not for a personal need to confess to assuage one's own guilt or for the need to retaliate in anger toward the other. Sometimes dalliances, attractions, even infidelities should be handled in private to find the source of the problem and then move on to repair the broken bond.

Why Infidelity Doesn't Work

- It runs counter to our cultural values.
- It's a betrayal of relationship trust.
- It deeply divides couples.

- It destroys our promise to be faithful.
- It can cause an enormous amount of pain.

Monogamy

- Creates and maintains trust.
- Upholds our relationship agreement.
- Creates peace and harmony.
- Adheres to a socially acceptable moral code.
- Supports relationship stability.
- Maintains intimacy.
- Supports safety and security.
- Maintains the emotional bond of truth and openness.

Monogamy is the gift we give to our partner and to ourselves. We don't feel good if we are not faithful. We feel bad when we hurt the ones we love. To feel truly connected, intimate, and loving, we need to feel safe from indiscretions. If we are attracted to someone else we must be allowed to think about it, but then let it go. We seek monogamy because it feels better, more connected, safe and intimate. If we find ourselves wanting to act out our attractions then we need to consult with a therapist in private to find the underlying causes. Just because we feel attracted doesn't mean we need to act on it. There is a logical reason for all behavior. We may need to dig deep to discover the reason behind our actions, but it's there. Finding it may lead us in a more positive direction in our relationship rather than creating pain.

Just because monogamy is difficult doesn't mean it's impossible. The challenge of being in a committed monogamous relationship is to become the kind of person we admire. Relationships raise the bar for behavior that is protective of the safety and security of monogamy. To be fully loving, caring, understanding and kind we must evolve; we must tussle with ourselves and our urges, our fantasies and our faults. There are no excuses in the real world. We have to rise up to be the best of ourselves, to maintain love by not creating pain and distrust.

9

Shame, Rage And Love-Making

We live in an atmosphere of shame. We are ashamed of everything that is real about us; ashamed of ourselves or our relatives, or our incomes, or our accents, or our opinions, or our experience, just as we are ashamed of our naked skins.

George Bernard Shaw, Man and Superman (1903)

Have you ever wondered why people behave as they do? What is it that makes us wary, defensive, incapable of loving, even brutal? How does early life experience affect the way we relate to others later on in life? To find answers to these questions we need to plunge below the surface.

Falling in love is magical. It's a potent force within us that stimulates our deepest longings, wishes, hopes and dreams. It can also cause pain and suffering. We may find ourselves re-living painful childhood experiences our current relationship. *The psychological term that best describes the effect of painful life experiences is the word "shame."* Shame wounds sustained early on can influence our present behavior in a variety of ways.

The word *shame* owes its origins to the Germanic root word "skem," which means to disgrace oneself. For centuries Indo-Europeans referred to shame as "kamm," meaning to cover or to hide. Shame, whether simply perceived as injurious or actually true, can be the root cause of conflicts within intimate relationships.

What may seem like a simple disagreement with our mate can have very complex origins. Shame is the term that best describes our reaction to humiliation or abuse. Shame wounds are about who we are because they're based on our belief that we are essentially worthless, weak, inadequate or bad. It is a core self concept that we are flawed and is most often held in secrecy, even from ourselves. We may believe we are a fraud, feel insecure or compensate for

our shameful self by behaving in ways that are the opposite from
how we really see ourselves. We may feel shy or act out angrily to
a small slight or try to be perfect.

Neurologist Sylvan Tompkins identified neural pathways in our
brain that are specifically targeted to shame. He discovered that
shame reactions are pre-wired into our brain. Shame is our personal
reaction to physical, sexual, and emotionally negative experiences
that are responses to acts of humiliation, rejection, abandonment,
or neglect. Interestingly, Tompkins found that shame and joy are
part of the same neural pathway in the brain. He believes that because of this connection between shame and joy we are especially
shame-prone when we're happy. Everyone at one time or another
experiences a shameful event in their lives. Shame is the feeling of
being cast out or that sinking feeling when we encounter the possibly being publically humiliated. Shame feelings can be generated
at any time in life but are especially powerful when we experience
them in childhood.

Something About Our Mind

Imagine our psyche as layered much like tree rings, constitut-
ing a catalogue of our experiences that are linked together in a
multi-dimensional tapestry of emotional and cognitive memories.
These rings are also linked to needs, hunger, and sexuality. So, in
a moment of humiliation the psyche will act like a phonograph record so when the needle hits the original experiential ring the old
tune starts playing in our body and mind. In one tenth of a second
(which is the speed of a brain wave) we will react, but with shame
our mind will instantly create a powerful defense like rage. Some
of these defenses include a sense of entitlement to retaliate or
turning the tables, aggression, to a complete shut down or fleeing
the scene. In a flash, our internal landscape changes, triggering an
intense negative response. If we can understand how experiences
from our past have influenced the way we respond to others we
can eventually change not only our reactions but the very core of
our being.

Shame wounds are caused by failures of empathy from parents, caregivers and loved ones. Empathy quite simply is the ability to put yourself in the other persons shoes. Infants and children have not fully developed an ability to empathize and therefore can't comprehend what's hurting them. They can't yet abstract so they can figure out who or what is hurting them they only know they are hurting. They experience everything as "me" including a shaming event. They are not able to understand why someone may be humiliating them, nor can they recognize what's causing it. Children respond to abuse as if their lives are threatened and their psyche closes ranks to protect them. At this point their survival instincts kick in and they will turn on themselves as opposed to expressing outrage toward the parent. They can't retaliate toward a rejecting parent for fear they will be pushed even further away. They don't understand what's happening to them, they only know that if feels bad. The brain is in charge of protecting them from harm so it steals away pain for safe keeping and shame along with it. These intense and severe experiences eventually exert influence over our behavior but from a separate place within the brain. From this isolated habitat within the self, defenses are formed as protection from further isolation, abandonment or humiliation.

What is the difference between shame and guilt? Where do they come from and what do they have to do with our sense of well being?

Shame vs. Guilt

Shame and guilt often occur together, yet they're different. Guilt is typically associated with our reaction to breaks in our moral or ethical behavior. We can feel as guilty about our thoughts as our actions. We may feel guilty about not doing things that we feel we "should" be doing. We can feel guilty about our dishonesty, greed, selfishness or being mean to someone we love. It's felt as a tearing away from our moral ideal for good behavior. Shame and guilt can be experienced at the same time: "I did something bad (guilt) and I did it because I'm bad (shame)."

Shame on You

The Talmud states that "Humiliation is worse than physical pain," and "Shaming another in public is like shedding blood." For children, shaming is unbearable and frightening. These bad experiences are interpreted by the child to be about a bad self. They also fear losing their parent's affection and acceptance. Out of terror and desperation to maintain their connection to the parent, the child must idealize them and devalue the self. This self-blaming creates a self-critical or antagonistic relationship within the self that can last throughout a lifetime. The parent is often a willing participant in this interchange because they may also blame the child. The pain and rage felt as a result of rejection and humiliation must be effectively concealed in order to preserve the fragile bond with the parent or caretaker. The child will react in a variety of ways to preserve the ideal parent for survival purposes either by trying to be what they think the parent wants them to be or by attacking the self.

Transformation

There is a direct relationship between potent shaming experiences during childhood and rage toward others later in life. When abused children mature and develop relationships of their own, their pent-up rage from these earlier shaming events will discharge during real or perceived conflicts. A man arrives home from a hellish day at work. His wife immediately hands him their baby and says "You take her; I'm so exhausted I can't see straight." His response will depend on how much shame/rage he is holding inside which may make him more shame-prone. Shame-prone is a description of someone who is loaded up inside with intense shame and is ready to blow. This shame material that has not been worked out is ready to produce rage. It may not take much, so an innocuous comment or request may elicit a rage response which may have little or nothing to do with the reality of the situation. If her husband had a humiliating experience earlier in the day, he will be more shame-prone and may become enraged at his wife's request: "Do you think I'm your slave? I work my ass off all day, and you have no appreciation for what I do. Instead you want me to take over your job as soon as I walk in the door; you're pathetic." This comment stimulates a transformation from a perceived humiliation, to shame and then to rage. His response will cause a break in their emotional connection and continued reactions like this may eventually end their relationship. It couldn't be more counterproductive, but the internal forces that produce this reaction are very powerful. To understand the difference between anger and rage we need to define what they mean so we can proceed to our discussion about how to resolve them.

Anger and Rage

Contrasting anger to rage is like comparing a rainstorm to a hurricane or a wave to a tsunami. Rage is a massive physical and psychic response to a shaming event, whereas anger is primarily a response to hurt feelings, sadness, fear, or guilt. In this sense anger is considered to be a secondary response to these conditions. Anger can be painful and counterproductive, but rage is violent and intended to injure as payback for a real or imagined offense. Rage is a most powerful human emotion and is largely responsible for what causes people to hurt, even murder each other.

Rage

The poet, psychoanalyst and post-trauma specialist Clarissa Pincola Estes writes that "Even raw and messy emotions are a form of light, crackling, bursting with energy. We can see that light of rage in a positive way, in order to see into places we cannot usually see."

Rage is an intense emotional state that is layered with both shameful feelings but also by complex defenses. Rage percolates like a pressure cooker in our body. It builds up inside and must find some way out. We observe in abusive relationships that it takes a very small stimulus to produce rage. It leaves their partner scratching their head trying to figure out what triggered it. A simple request to pass the potatoes can turn into a violent episode when the pain from shame has built up inside. As tragic emotional memories become too intense for the system to hold onto, our brain creates a way out through entitlement to rage. In its own way rage is an attempt at empathy but it's the "I'll show you" kind of revenge mentality so it's only about the person who is experiencing it, not about the other person. The problem is that only one person is a part of this one way empathy. Even if the intention is for the other person to know how we feel, it always breaks the emotional bond and re-creates the earlier shaming event. Rage can serve as an intense connection and may be the only way certain couples can connect. Through rage they are locked in a violent struggle that is quite extreme while it's going on. The aftermath is broken hearts, distrust and contempt.

The other intentions of rage are to change, to get through or to transform the other. The desire to change or transform the other person through rage changes nothing for the better. Rage as an attempt to make the other person change is a self deception, not only for the purpose of expulsion but for the deep desire to injure or seek revenge. The person who rages cannot control it and may have no idea where it's really coming from. The early idealized relationship with brutal parent is now being re-enacted in the new relationship, so the victim has now become the aggressor.

Anger

When children witness angry scenes between their parents and other family members, they may believe that expressing anger is a normal part of relationship life. As with shame, if anger was a consistent theme at home, it will reappear in all important relationships. For couples, anger causes more problems than it solves. Anger and conflict are normal. It's not that we *get* angry; it's *how* we get angry that is critical to relationships. Because anger is a result of hurt feelings, sadness, guilt and emotional pain, it may be more complex than we think it is. So when we get angry the first thing we need to do is to stop, cool off and think about what's actually making us angry. It may take some time to figure out the source, but when we know what's causing our anger we are in a much better place to resolve it.

A Buddhist monk was asked about anger. His response was, "Don't suppress it, but don't express it." What he meant was, don't push anger down; understand where it's coming from, but hold onto it until you know what it is and can talk about it with an even temper. Learning to communicate what we are angry about without expressing our anger takes self reflection, practice, time and patience. Again, self knowledge helps us understand what it is that makes us angry and why. This leads to being able to be more accepting of our mate and ourselves which can be a resource for a deeper intimacy. When couples can be observant about where their anger is coming from and what it's telling them about what they truly want and need from each other they are actively creating intimacy.

Where Does it Come From?

How does shame create rage? Is it something that we can change or does it remain a part of our system? Children respond in much the same way to the same kinds of experiences. If they are given a voice, are understood, cared for, listened to and loved, they will become that way as adults. If they are neglected they will feel worthless. If they are beaten they will feel they are bad. If they are sexually abused they will feel guilty and bad. If children are yelled at and criticized they will yell and criticize themselves as adults. Another form of shame is evidenced when children feel they have destroyed family bliss because their parents fought bitterly about them. The bad feeling they get from those kinds of arguments form into a shame identity: "I feel bad; therefore I am bad." The child cannot interpret what their feelings are telling them about others but instead take them in as part of the self. The child does not try to think this way, but the brain will automatically interpret bad experience as bad self.

Noted psychiatrist Dr. M.J. Barry describes the early shame experience:

Shame originates from the parent's attitude toward the child, being an angry rejection of the child himself. The parent attacks the child's right to their behavior and degrades the child. This is usually followed by an angry rejection of the child. The child through similar onslaughts is forced into the humiliating feeling that they are worth less than the parent is worth. They fear abandonment, they fear their own anger and resentment, and they suffer the loss of confidence in their own reactions or the ability to control their rage. The distance that the parent creates from their rejection of the child because of his/her badness leaves the child alone in painful solitude.

What Dr. Barry is describing may appear as a temper tantrum that is quite normal for that developmental stage and is just a phase the child is going through. A child may not know how to ask for affection, and because the parent has not provided a method to express his needs, he will fall into a tantrum as a last-ditch effort to get the attention he craves. His parents may decide to correct the "bad" behavior by rejecting or punishing him for what may actually be a cry for help. The child may connect his needs for affection and attention to this shameful experience and feel humiliated. Then in adulthood he will have a very difficult time expressing his needs for affection and attention and will rage at his partner for not knowing how to respond.

Importantly, we need to know what happened to us and then we must go about making important distinctions between our experience and who we are. This is the first stage of becoming who we are. We must also understand what realistic expectations for ourselves and others really are. How can we get our needs met so we can feel filled up inside? This can be a very complex process and must be done with another person who is either a mentor or therapist. If we didn't have a dialogue with our parents about what our feelings mean then how are we supposed to know what they are telling us about ourselves and our mate?

Going Way Back

Ten thousand years ago if a child was left alone for more than a few minutes, he would have become lunch for a wild animal. Our brain still functions like we are living ten thousand years ago. So it reacts to isolation, rejection, or abandonment as if it were life-threatening. Our internal survival system takes whatever measures it needs to insure our continued survival. The brain will conjure up psychological defenses to protect us from what it perceives to be life threatening even though it may not be. Our defenses are hard wired from past experience into our thought processes and can shift reality to fit the defense. For example we may feel fear whenever we're alone and not know that what we are feeling is abandonment terror. A baseline anxiety or fear has formed that is based on something that has actually happened. .

There are a vast number of defenses that are based on fears of abandonment or humiliation. They might look like the compulsion to be perfect, depression, anxiety, or attention-getting devices like rage and hysteria. We may twist what others say to fit our need to feel righteous or we may just pull way back and not trust that anyone can be there for us. We may be angry on the inside and people pleasing on the outside to maintain a sense of approval. This fits within the framework of internal shame. These behaviors are all meant to maintain connections with others and to be well thought of. All defenses, from being right, to being outright defensive are the way our mind protects our shame from being exposed. Shame wounds feel the same as physical injuries except we can't see them and our mind hides them from us as well. The larger the emotional wound the greater the defenses that will be required to defend against anything that might stimulate the pain.

More About Survival

Infants and children distract themselves from loneliness through fantasy. Painful experiences also increase our need for fantasy as a way of coping with powerful feelings that can't be understood. For the system to operate effectively, the psyche must create massive shifts in reasoning, either in fantasy or by twisting reality to expel pain. Only when we can to see clearly into our protective system will we be able to unravel its complexity and see what is causing our behavior.

Rage appears to the person experiencing it as if it's really about the other. They have sinned and they must pay. Psychologists refer to this need for revenge as "talionic," a reference to the first rule of law enacted in Babylonia about 2,000 BC when King Hammurabi called for "an eye for an eye, and a tooth for a tooth." This code was known as the "judgment of righteousness." Rage feels justified to the person experiencing it. *Rage is the way our shame wound expels its pain.*

When I first heard stories of raging spouses or partners blocking the doorway so they couldn't leave just so they could continue raging, I was confused. When they came to therapy sessions, they would agree to take time-outs, but in the thick of battle a different scenario emerged. The difference in an individual during a raging episode and when they aren't is significant. Rage builds from the force of internalized pain until in an orgy of emotion it blasts out, an awesome reminder of the original primal scene.

The interesting quality about rage that makes it so difficult to modify or change is that the reality distortion causing the person to feel entitled to rage is so real to them. They perceive rejection or humiliation even when it doesn't actually exist. Many a perpetrator has beaten his significant other on an assumption that was entirely based on a primal distortion. There are occasions when there is actually a stimulating event causing the rage but rage always causes more injury. Shame/rage/violence is not just the providence of men; women also perpetrate rage to their spouses and children. Men are most often the offenders but they do not have an exclusive hold on it. The major problem in controlling rage is how incredibly powerful it is. Until the wound that causes rage is healed the problem with rage will remain.

How Our Mind Tries to Help

Paradoxically, shame and rage are the most powerful human emotions and are governed by a part of the brain that thinks it's helping us to survive but in reality it's only creating more pain. In all of this, people are often only marginally aware of the consequences of their behavior or where it may be coming from. Stuart

Yudofsky, M.D. writes in *Fatal Flaws*, a book about personality and character disorders:

> Although their causes and presentations are often hidden and confusing, flawed personalities and character structures create wreckage that is not at all subtle. The resulting pain and suffering can overwhelm the lives of those with whom they are importantly associated; and the related material losses are incalculable. Examples include your fiancée being unfaithful; your husband gambling away the savings for the children's college tuition; your employee stealing money from your business; your parent being abused by an attendant in a nursing home; your child attending school while on drugs; your wife injuring herself and others while driving while intoxicated.

Yudofsky goes on to describe that these people truly believe they don't have a problem, and therefore feel that it's not necessary to make changes in their behavior. As we can see, their mind has created a powerful defense to insure that the method for expelling pain from their wound is intact. What he's saying here is that we may be thinking one thing consciously but our unconscious mind directs us to do something quite different. We may not want to gamble, drink, do drugs, beat our mate, or steal from our boss, but it still happens. The origins and causes for these behaviors are multifaceted and often bear little relation to rational thought. The brain wants to protect us, so alcohol, drugs and stealing may serve to take the pain away. What therapists try to do is to combine rational thought with our need to protect ourselves. In this way we enlist our mind to determine what our body is telling us. Shame is a primary distortion of what we believe to be our true self. We may feel inadequate but reality tells us that all living things have worth. We all have value and purpose in this world. Only by developing a vocabulary for our emotional wounds can we learn to understand them and know how they affect our thoughts and behavior. In this way we will be able to express our deeply held desires for love and connection.

The Steps to Understanding Anger and Rage

- Look, see and understand the internal messages your body sends you that reveal your personal mythology.
- Fill this understanding with compassion, respect, and empathy for who you are.
- Develop an internal voice of reason to counteract the negative thoughts and feelings.
- Learn how to distinguish your real or true self from the distorted inadequate self.
- Separate your personal myth (weak, worthless, inadequate) from the way you really are.
- Learn how to relieve yourself of self blame by utilizing positive self-talk.
- Develop the ability to understand and rectify your relationship distortions as the key that unlocks the door to creating a lasting intimacy.
- Remember that self knowledge is one component for maintaining intimacy and the willingness to look at the other from their perspective is the other part.
- Find a mentor, therapist or enlist your mate as a helper in this process.

Self-Talk

When we can understand that what's wrong with us is that we *think* something is wrong with us, only then can we begin the process of neutralizing our inner distortion. First, we need to consider what is actually true about who we truly are, something like "If I do my best that will have to be enough." We can use self-talk to not only articulate our personal myth but also to debunk it. The intention is to separate myth from reality. Let's take a typical personal myth that says "No one is going to like me at this party." Then, we say to our self, "that's not true. It's not up to me it's up to them to decide if they like me." What I can do is to be true to myself and see what happens." Like "Hey, this is me, like or lump it." You can try out different ideas and concepts to see which one works best. I remember one morning saying to myself that "all I can do is all I can do" and I found this to be very relieving to my worry that I would overwhelmed by a busy week. Self-talk should be tailored to fit what works best to neutralize our self-distortion.

The steps to neutralizing negative personal myths is to first think about what our myth is telling us, then what the reality is and then what we need to do to fit our thinking into a true sense of reality. We will need these steps from time to time to take our distortion away.

A White Wedding

Jennie and Jack had been married ten years when they arrived for their first session. They had two children within the first three years of marriage. The stress it created caused frequent violent arguments. Their fights were centered on child-rearing and money. Their language at these times was filled with insults and personal recriminations. They were exhausted from all the fighting. They couldn't break out of the negative cycle. Clues to the cause of their rage began to emerge during our therapy sessions.

Jennie had developed a career as an advertising executive and Jack worked as a computer analyst. Jack worked from home and Jennie drove to various projects throughout the city. She was a workaholic, frequently showing up late for planned activities, which infuriated Jack.

Jennie grew up in a household with a distant, intellectual, and perfectionist father and a rather overworked career woman mother. She felt like her mother opted out of her life while her father demanded excellence. There was nowhere to hide from his verbally abusive tirades, and her mother was nowhere to be found. To cope with her father she had to internalize her anger and become as perfect as possible to mollify him.

When Jennie got out into the world she discovered that she was more like her parents than she had imagined. She observed herself working too much like her mother and having exceedingly high expectations for herself and others, just like her father. When she felt angry with her husband or others she quietly seethed, and then would show up late or forget things just as she had done with her father to make him angry. Never being able to live up to her father's expectations fueled her need to overcompensate, to be perfect. Her perfectionism resulted in her running behind schedule frequently and caused her not to leave home until everything was just so. Her lateness caused many fights with Jack, who felt that she did it because she didn't care about him. After many such incidents, Jack would demean Jennie for what he believed was a lack of concern for her family. Jennie would sit for a long time and after reaching a boiling point she would storm out of the house. After serious and protracted fights, there would be a period of calm and then the negative cycle would begin again. They were tired of the repetitive process and wanted to work out a better way.

Our first point of entry was to understand what their rage was about and what it was doing for them. When they raged Jack had her complete attention that he couldn't get otherwise. Jenny could use Jack's criticism as an excuse to release her pent-up anger. His rage made him feel powerful instead of helpless.

As we looked closely at Jack's family dynamic, we exposed the cause of his rage. It turned out that Jack's cold, critical and withholding mother was the cause of his low self- esteem and anger toward Jenny. She was an old-fashioned disciplinarian who was emotionally and physically abusive toward him as a child. She ran a tight ship with little room for Jack's big personality. Jack's father was a traveling salesman and was often on the road; when he was home, he was remote and preoccupied. Jack felt invisible. He was largely unaware how his experiences with his mother and father had affected his reactions to Jennie.

Jack and Jennie's negative cycle was a response to the way they related to their own families. It was all they knew. Jack didn't feel that Jennie loved him or cared about his concerns so he raged and emotionally abused her just like his mother did to him. He didn't want to depend on her for his emotional needs because he was afraid that she would reject him. He hid under his righteous superiority. In their arguments, Jack became commanding and critical, thereby making Jennie feel stupid and inadequate. Jennie raged at him for being righteous and superior, and Jack would rage about her tardiness, irresponsibility and lack of concern for the family, especially him. Rage was a safer way to connect. When they could see what they were doing and why, they began to make changes in the way they related their needs and feelings to each other.

They agreed to make time for each other. They stopped being reactive and began to actively express their desires and upsets without being condescending or passive aggressive. They began the journey to find kinder and more productive ways to become intimate and to be truly emotionally connected. They no longer needed rage to find a connection. They learned that understanding where they were coming from allowed them to be more compassionate, empathic, and tender. This knowledge gave them the connection they longed for and needed.

Entitlement to Rage

Learning to work through rage begins with understanding the entitlement to rage. Entitlement is the key that unlocks the door to shame and rage. It's not so much a thought process as it is a defensive/reactive state. Anger and rage run through the conduit of entitlement. It's the feeling of *"You hurt me so I'm going to hurt you"*. Understanding entitlement is the first step to breaking down unproductive conflicts. Entitlement is at the heart of most raging dysfunctional couple conflict.

The way to stop the need for entitlement is to heal the wound that necessitates such a response. So much domestic violence is based on entitlement to rage. To deconstruct entitlement is difficult because of the power that the unconscious holds over our behavior. The supremacy of the rage response to any conscious thought is what makes it so difficult to control. In spite of our best intentions rage rules our system. The most important part of letting go of entitlement is to embrace the need to let it go. As we have discussed, rage builds in a pressure cooker deep within our psyche. We need to completely accept the problem with rage. Then, we need to heal the core of what drives the rage. To define ourselves differently is what is necessary.

Most people don't understand how their defenses work because they can't see them. If we feel attacked, we defend. It's difficult to remain calm and think of a positive way to respond when we feel hurt by someone we love. We are flooded with rage. The patience required to sit down with our partner and tell them how they've hurt us is not easy because rage is like a wall of pain. Our first reaction is to strike back. The righteousness and "correctness" of entitlement is potent and engaging. Entitlement is not the problem, shame is. Healing shame must be an ongoing process to correct what is untrue. Shame can be either intellectual or deeply emotional or both. To heal it we must be aware of it at all times. Then when it expresses itself we need to neutralize it by firmly affixing reality thinking to the distortion. The most difficult task it to know what reality is. That often takes discussion with others to understand. Asking our mate, our elders, or our therapist about what they see is the key to helping ourselves.

A patient and I were discussing her issues when, in the process of explaining to her that she becomes infuriated whenever she feels disconnected, she became irritated and, yes, infuriated. Having worked together for some time, we were able to piece it together, and she was finally able to understand how it worked. In the past she had angrily left our sessions and then at our next visit would explain to me how I had behaved so terribly the week before. She felt entitled to take me to task over my perceived infractions. When she could see how her sense of entitlement was about needing to feel important and listened to, she began to express herself in a more positive way.

We all know people who feel like they have a free pass to act badly, as if there were no consequences. Amazingly, they can't figure out why their mate doesn't want to be with them when they've raged at them so mightily. As we observe this behavior it's hard to understand why someone who wants love, care and support would rage as a means of getting it. Their behavior creates the exact opposite of what they raging about. The force of shame on our psyche is so powerful that it creates devastation where love should be. The trouble is we can't see how our shame system is working or know what to do when it blows up. It's a sad commentary when relationships begin with such hope and then are destroyed by rage.

Taking the Pain Away

All efforts to eliminate rage will fail until the cause of it is determined. Since shame is so heavily defended, it can be quite a challenge to find the core. A new approach to modern medicine is referred to as "functional medicine." The focus of functional medicine is to search for the cause of the illness so the cure will be lasting, as opposed to treating symptoms only. It's the same in psychology. Unless the cause for behavior is determined, it will persist. While treating depression, anxiety, poor self-esteem, and relationship problems, we often find that shame is the core issue.

Rage emanating from shame is essentially a paranoid process because it is directed toward the other and originates from a shame wound. In a paranoid process, even before the person is conscious of the feeling, the shame has already been projected outward. Paranoid means that bad feelings about the self are propelled outward to become bad "other." Persecutory inner thoughts or feelings toward the self are thrown out of the system and reappear as dangerous or negative outer images, causing us to see our mate as a part of our internal shame. This should not be confused with paranoid personality disorder which is much more severe in nature.

Neutralizing shame requires that we work through our self-criticism and self-blame, feel more compassionate about our past and allow ourselves to grieve over losses. Taking time to consider our needs and feelings will help us take better care of ourselves. All this is a critical piece for easing the pain of shame. Being physically active and creating a healthy relationship with ourselves is one of the best methods of neutralizing bad self-feelings. The problem with shame is that it is negative and creates depression and anxiety that make it difficult to feel good about ourselves.

A Battle-Weary Couple

Ben's parents were Holocaust survivors. They were continually terrified and anxious, so much so that they could not provide the emotional support or nurturing that young Ben needed. They worked long hours and were frequently too exhausted to pay much attention to him. He eventually came to the realization that being a good boy, always helping, and being perfect, were the best ways to get attention and approval. His parents were capable of approval, but were completely shut down emotionally and unable to express love. Ben resented his needs for affection because his parents were not emotionally able to give it. He felt humiliated by his desire for love. He was enraged that his needs were of so little concern to his parents. In his child's mind, he could not comprehend that his parents were too traumatized and tired to give him the love he craved. He couldn't get what he wanted, so he had to earn what emotional crumbs he could get by being the little helper. Underneath the good boy was an angry, sometimes raging child.

Ben and Susan entered therapy in crisis. When I asked Ben about his childhood, he said he couldn't remember much of it. But he eventually began to describe a life of loneliness and heartache. He detailed his efforts to be a good son. His compassion for his parents' plight and his devaluation of his needs for love and affection created an internal wall. In this way he was unable to value his own pain. While in college, Ben's repressed neediness caused him to chase after women to get them to want him, but when they did he rejected them. He would devalue them for being inferior and stupid. The best way to not need someone is to devalue them. So, the shame that was linked to his needs caused him to devalue others so he didn't have to feel the pain. As he got older, he felt the desire to get married. It was about this time that he met Susan.

Susan's father was a successful businessman who was seldom home. When he was, the house was filled with unreasonable expectations and anger. Her mother eventually found solace in alcohol and prescription drugs. Susan, like Ben, tried to be a perfect child to please her father and to keep her mother from turning to drugs. Her anger at her parents had to be withdrawn in order to receive what little affection and attention there was to go around. On the surface she was very nice, but an inferno of repressed rage was seething underneath.

When Ben and Susan began dating, they adopted the good/girl good/boy behaviors they had mastered as children. After they married, the rage that was lying just below the surface blew open. They were shaken by the intensity of their tempers. When they first entered therapy they described a scene where Susan had promised Ben a romantic candlelit dinner, but when he arrived home he found her sitting on the sofa chatting with a friend. Ben felt humiliated; it was clear that she did not care about him. He fumed until the friend left and then flew into a rage, yelling, "How dare you!" Susan couldn't believe that her husband was reacting this way over a friend coming over and dinner being late. She retaliated, "Are you crazy?" Ben felt humiliated, yelling, "You don't give a damn about anyone but yourself." He began berating her with a laundry list of injustices. Then she lunged at him. The flailing and screaming that ensued caused the neighbors to call the police.

To thoroughly fathom Ben and Susan's interaction we need only look at their history. Ben's shame was linked to his dependency needs. His rage originated from his experience of rejected needs. When their marriage was shattered by rage, they could see that something disturbing and powerful was happening, and they needed to understand how it worked it if they were ever to have a healthy relationship.

Ben and Susan felt entitled to criticize and blame each other. After all, it was the fault of the other person for failing to be perfect. In the beginning of our therapy we focused on understanding that their behavior was causing substantial emotional pain for both of them. We embarked on a search to find the source of the rage. We discovered that their rage was related to their mutual sense of insignificance.

Ben and Susan worked out some interventions that helped them bring their issues into the present so they could talk about them. They began by practicing time-outs when they became angry. Then they created a strategy that included reflecting on the principle they were trying to talk about without getting bogged down on who said what to whom. They tried to talk about what they wanted in the future from each other and to think about what personal issue was being stimulated during disagreements. They considered empathy when they worked on a conflict. They learned to check out and verbalize their negative fantasies and then work toward understanding what was happening in real time. Finally, they mobilized a working process to decipher their emotional wounds well enough so that they could identify them when they were upset. In this way they began to learn how to steer clear of behaviors that triggered their rage.

Is It Nature or Nurture?

The age old question still lingers as to whether we are born the way we are or become who we are based on experience. Except for those who suffer from conditions like bipolar disorder, attention deficit hyperactive disorder and schizophrenia that are due to chemical imbalances, most of us are born with a tendency toward a certain temperament and constitution. How we are affected by experience by and large is very similar. Because our experiences are never exactly the same, we are in many ways quite different. Neural pathways that form personality are developed entirely from experience. David Keirsey writes in *Please Understand Me*, "People are different in fundamental ways. They want different things; they have different motives, purposes, aims, values, needs, drives, impulses, urges. Nothing is more fundamental than that. They believe differently; they think, cogitated, conceptualize, perceive, understand, comprehend, and cogitate differently. And of course, manners of acting and emoting, governed as they are by wants and beliefs, follow suit and differ radically among people." The fundamental challenge in relationships is to balance those differences fairly and equally between each other, and most importantly to develop a process for doing it.

Attachment

When we consider shame and rage it requires that we also understand what our early attachments to our parents were like.

Currently in the community of psychologists and psychotherapists there is a great deal of interest in attachment theory. Attachment theory was originally developed by the renowned British psychiatrist John Bowlby. He studied the way infants and toddlers did or did not attach to their parents, specifically the mother. He characterized attachment styles as secure, anxious, ambivalent, avoidant or more recently a new term was added, disorganized and confused.

Attachment pioneer Mary Ainsworth developed a study that she called the "Strange Situation," using toddlers to demonstrate different attachment styles. The toddler was led into a room with a stranger. The mother would talk to the stranger for ten minutes and at that time the toddler was free to interact with the stranger as well. The mother would then leave the room, and the toddler and the stranger would be left alone. After ten to fifteen minutes the mother would re-enter the room to interact or soothe the toddler. Then the mother would be observed to determine the way she interacted with her child.

The "Strange Situation" provided two methods for determining the attachment style of the toddler, one with a stranger and the other with the mother. Through this a consistent pattern of attachment was revealed. The securely attached toddlers were more able to feel secure with the stranger. The toddlers whose attachments were not secure were anxious and upset. Those who were ambivalent or avoidant did not respond either to the stranger or the mother leaving the room. Watching how they behaved when the mother left and when she returned gave the observers vital information about the levels of security or the lack of it in their attachment styles. From her studies, Ainsworth developed her ideas further by describing how attachment styles can form combinations like anxious/avoidant, or ambivalent/avoidant, or anxious/ambivalent or disorganized.

Attachment theory is a way of defining the quality of emotional connections that we form early in life and helps us to understand the influence they have had on all our intimate relationships. For example if we felt anxious about our attachment to our parents we will feel the same anxiety in all subsequent intimate relationships. By the same token with if we felt ambivalent and avoidant attachments early on then all future relationships will have these features.

In this sense shame and attachment are different ways of defining how early connectedness or the lack of it influences our sense of self. Shame and rage are founded on very poor attachment with the parent. Neglect and abuse create intense rage that are a response to severed attachments as children and continue to break attachments as adults. In all rage states there is a desire to attach through rage. We so often see couples raging about what they are not getting from the other and yet that very process makes it impossible to get.

Should We Blame the Parents?

The problem of blaming the parents remains a thorny issue for psychotherapists and patients because of our need to be loyal to the parents and lay the responsibility for our problems on some essential flaw within us. Parents invariably try to do their best but they may not provide the necessary emotional connections, support, or nurturing needed by their child and as a result may unintentionally hurt them. Most parents are doing what they have learned from their parents and that may be limited or even abusive. As we understand that a series of painful experiences created our negative self-image, we can eventually build a true sense of who we are. Not that we must reject or even confront our parents, but in accepting them as human beings we humanize them and ourselves. Most parents didn't have such an easy time of it and were doing what they thought was best.

Shame and self-blame are intertwined. Understanding how self-blaming is toxic to our relationships is a necessary step in the process of developing emotional health. Self-blame or self-loathing is the way children react to abuse. The key point of reference in looking at what role our caretakers played in our identity formation, or the lack of it, is not necessarily to blame them or use them to excuse our behavior, but to understand how they affected us. Understanding our history not only helps us alleviate self-blame, criticism, depression, anxiety, and violence but also provides important insights into the workings of our present intimate relationships. Parents not only provide positive influences but they have their own personal issues as well. If a parent is a positive person, it will rub off on their children. By the same token, if parents have low self-esteem, they will pass it on. We identify with our parents and in that sense we psychologically take them in as positive and/or negative aspects of ourselves. They live within us and become our own inner voice.

Whatever we do not understand about ourselves and our past will be transported into our present. If we deny our essential wounds, they will surface without our knowledge and drive a wedge into our relationships with others. Our understanding of what has shaped us allows us to make contact with the love that lies just beneath. Understanding what we feel, want and need makes it more possible to be intimate with our mate. This awareness allows us to distinguish between ourselves and our mate so when disputes do arise we can understand what our contribution to the problem actually is.

The term 'It takes a village to raise a child" was made famous by Hillary Clinton but is actually an old African saying. But in the jungle of every day life even very competent and caring parents can be completely overwhelmed by sick children, depression, marital issues and a host of difficulties that make it hard to pay attention to their children. For thousands of years children were raised in tribes or clans. Our psyche is still based on the need for consistent and available contact with care takers. To grow up in a two or often one parent home is woefully insufficient to the needs of most children. When grandparents, aunts, uncles, and support groups are present, children fare much better. It's not that mothers and fathers are bad per se, but there may not be enough emotional food to go around, and children suffer for it. Take for instance a two-parent household with an autistic child. The child with the disability will take up most of the space and the "normal" child may fall through the cracks. The healthier child may be more prone to self esteem problems as an adult, and may feel that his or her needs for affection are bad. Other family issues like alcoholism, job loss, injury, health, and their financial situation all influence children and their sense of who they are.

Making Connections

When psychologists ponder the psyche, they are most interested in studying the causes of psychological conflicts and what promotes healing. Their main focus is on what it means to be healthy, and specifically what may be preventing people from actualizing their potential or true self. In evaluating what causes inhibition, anxiety and depression, we need to compare that to a model of health, intelligence, biological imbalances, age, friends, teachers, and catastrophic events. The reason we look to family and childhood as a basis for psychological health is that children spend so much time with their parents and siblings when they are the most sensitive, dependent and vulnerable. If we can take the negative out of blame and connect the cause with the effect, then we shift from *self-blaming* to a *cause and effect* reality that's based on the experiences that have made us the way we are.

Leon Wurmser writes in his classic study *The Mask of Shame* that the child is an "omnipotent masochist" because he feels responsible for causing his own pain. If his parents were cold and withholding, he experiences this as, "I am inadequate and unlovable." If his parents were angry and rejecting, he will believe that he is bad and useless. If his parents punished him for being angry or left him alone, he will be forced to hold in his anger and direct it at himself in a quest for perfection and redemption in his parents' eyes. If his parents were fragile and he happens to be angry, this fragility might cause him to withhold his anger or deny it altogether.

Gershon Kaufman writes in *The Meaning of Shame,* "Even though the aftermath of shame can be severe, the way to a self-affirming identity yet lies in the deeply human capacity to be fully restored, in the knowledge that one individual can restore the interpersonal bridge with another however late it may be and in the awareness that human relationships are repairable. Through such restoring of the bridge, shame is transcended." This quote expresses the central theme of what it means to be human. When we experience concern, interest, and caring, we're affected positively, and this is what restores our true nature. If it's uncaring people who inflict wounds, then we need loving people to heal them. In this process we see what love and care from others means to our lives and for our very soul.

Battle Royale

Bob and June had lived together for five years when they first came to see me. Bob complained about June's temper and described their dramatic fights, which had culminated in several breakups. One night June arrived home to find Bob engrossed in a phone conversation. During one of their reconciliations they had agreed that when one of them came home the other one would stop what they were doing and say hello before they resumed their previous activity. When June got home she gave Bob a signal to please acknowledge her, which he ignored. She went from a slow burn to rage. When he finally did stop talking, they battled, each accusing the other of being mean and insensitive. Their fights were an established pattern in their relationship, so we needed to look below the surface.

June was a child of divorce and had little or no contact with her father. When she was five, her mother remarried, focusing much of her attention on her new husband and the child they had soon thereafter. June felt her mother became even more disinterested in her as she spent most of her time with her new husband and their baby. June felt abandoned. She believed her mother rejected her because she was insignificant.

June grew into a beautiful and sought-after woman. She defended against exposing her shame about herself by not letting anyone get close to her. She became fickle, demanding, and judgmental toward her suitors. Her personal sense of unimportance was disguised by her independence and idealism. She created a perfect man fantasy as a defense against her fear of abandonment. She projected this ideal onto her boyfriends and they always came up short. When a lover failed in some way, she felt justified in her rejection of him. This enabled her to feel superior instead of valueless. When she met Bob, she felt that she had finally met her ideal man. He was kind and loving toward her at first, but eventually he became angry and critical.

Bob was the product of an iron-fisted father and a passive mother. His anger at authority made Bob resist being told what to do. The idea of someone controlling him was particularly offensive. His dictatorial father never allowed him to express his feelings and pressured him into being obedient. He also taught Bob that expressing feelings was a sign of weakness. The father's fierce anger made it impossible for Bob to express his anger toward him, so he found a more passive means of expressing it. He vowed never to speak to his father unless spoken to, which vexed and angered his father to no end.

On the night in question Bob knew that June wanted to make contact with him. When June came in and wanted him to get off the phone, it triggered his rage at authority, and he ignored her, causing June to feel invisible, triggering her rage. He chose to stay on the phone as a passive means of expressing his anger. Feelings cannot be effectively hidden and will inevitably find their way out. In finding the source of his anger, Bob's inner wounds emerged. With a great deal of soul searching he learned how his unacknowledged anger was expressing itself.

By understanding her own conflict with dependency, June could more easily conceptualize how to express her needs directly. She understood that her early experience of rejection affected her behavior in the present. Bob recognized that he had difficulty expressing anger and learned to be more direct with his feelings about being told what to do. Accepting what made them the way they were enabled them to find healthier solutions to their arguments. Only through working out the sources of their rage could they begin to build a truly intimate relationship. Once they knew what was hurting them, they could make more positive choices.

The Human Condition

We exist in an internal sea of multilayered experiences mixed with impulses like need, sexuality and hunger all swimming in emotions, thoughts, desires and fears. When we add another person to the mix we are increasing the complexity by a factor of ten. To make matters even more complicated, we create expectations, moral beliefs, and defenses that run parallel and are entwined with each other. This intricate set of impulses, reactions, thoughts and impressions forms our inner world. All of these processes influence our personality and mood. Our smart defenses can easily trick us into believing something that we deem to be true is not. The ability of our survival system to develop incredible rationales, to form complex defenses, and then to make us so totally believe in them is truly awesome and deeply human.

To enjoin our personality with another and to develop and maintain a loving relationship is challenging at best. The goal is to determine who we are and what we want through examination of the truth that lies within. The ability to form loving attachments is what feeds us and makes us whole.

Tough as Love

The pressures that couples face in our modern culture are like no other in history. The fallout from current stresses and violent confrontations are a part of our lives, and we witness this continually on the streets and in the news. The demand for wages to keep up with rising prices, the competition for jobs, urban alienation, and the threat of terrorism are just some of the reasons for collective angst. Our inability to develop and maintain a loving relationship amidst these prevailing trends adds even more strain to our all-too-taxing lives.

As couples face more obstacles than ever before, the pressure from stress, competition and life can seriously impact our connections with our loved ones. Anger and rage are the most serious reactions to the difficulty of life. Angry couples become entangled in a negative cycle that may eventually kill even the most intense loving relationship. As we are caught up in the struggle for survival and success we are vulnerable to the shame that may come from not feeling able to compete in the workplace or the stress of doing so. By the time we learn that the very struggle for fame or fortune frequently adds more stress and less happiness, it may be too late. The aftermath of the search for success is frequently painful and lonely. Hopefully, we can learn from such experiences, so that our sense of success and value includes the balance of relationships and family.

There are certain processes that create and make love, and there are others that destroy love. If we use the anagram CURE and then attach words, the key to Love-Making: *From the Inside Out* emerges. To heal our shame wounds, we need to use CURE to form a positive process within and between each other.

Compassion - toward others and ourselves.

Understanding - where we came from and who we are.

Respect - for our struggle.

Empathy - toward others and ourselves.

Our childhood is a permanent record, a system unto itself. But we don't have to be imprisoned by it. Once we understand how our deepest shame issues have affected the way we see ourselves and others, we are free to make choices about the way we want to live our lives. Knowledge is power, and this power creates the freedom to make positive choices about the way we want to be. We can choose a life of loving kindness and compassion if we define our lives this way. *We cannot change experience, but we can change our relationship to it.*

10

Couples Who Beat The Odds

But you and I, love, we are together,
from our clothes down to our roots,
together in the autumn, in water, in hips,
until we can be alone together, only you, only me.

Pablo Neruda
From Sonnet II, *One Hundred Love Sonnets*

Couples who beat the odds are active, engaged, committed, and are able to accept each other's influence, especially in times of stress and conflict. This dynamic process includes tolerance, patience, fairness, a sense of humor, and a willingness to be flexible with emotionally charged issues. People who are easygoing tend to let small spats roll off their backs and are able to bounce back from irritations and differences. Those who expect that love will conquer all or believe that their relationship is bulletproof are in for a surprise. Couples who beat the odds make their relationship a high priority and create time and space for tending to each other's needs. These couples strive to craft a relationship that is continually moving toward support and contentment. When couples know what they want from each other and the direction they're going, they're actively creating their own sense of excitement and possibility.

There are specific abilities and values that successful couples seem to possess. They have gained them through a dynamic approach that includes personal insight, acknowledgement, and being able to include the perspective of the other. What follows are some practical concepts for couples who want to beat the odds.

Money Money Money

Couples fight about money more than any other issue: how to spend it, who's spending it, who earns it, who's spending too much, what belongs to whom, and for what reasons. Money seems to be the one thing that no one likes to talk about. Money is important to us; it's like air, we need it. Most people develop their relationship to money from their experience growing up. If their family was very poor and they become rich they may still have the same fears as when they were poor. A friend of mine grew up very poor, but became wealthy. He bought a very expensive car but would drive around to five different stores looking for the best price on tomatoes. On the other hand, if someone grows up rich and becomes poor they may still spend like they have money. Money can also temporarily make people feel adequate, worthwhile, powerful and emotionally secure.

Many people have very little discretionary income and this affects everything they do. Money limitation is stressful and people will even go into deep credit card debt when they can't stand the lack of freedom that their relative poverty presents. Financial problems can influence the well-being of a relationship. The inability to afford gifts, travel, fun and special occasions can affect self-esteem and can create depression and anxiety. This situation is even more intensified when there is difficulty meeting basic needs like food, shelter, and medical attention. All this takes an emotional toll in long-term relationships.

What Money Can't Do

Arthur Stone, Vice-Chairman of the Department of Psychiatry at Stony Brook University, New York, has done extensive research on the subject of money and concluded that money in itself does not make people happy. He writes in the prestigious journal *Science*:

It's mostly illusory. When you look at people's actual experience, the rich are not happier than others, and if they are it has nothing to do with the money they have. Having a lot of money or a big house has little to do with a person's overall mood.

Stone uses variable techniques for understanding people's attitudes about money. He concludes, along with Daniel Kahneman, who won a Nobel Prize in Economic Sciences, that people tend to exaggerate the benefits of an imagined gain in wealth. He stresses,

Increases in income have been found to have mainly a transitory effect on individuals' reported life satisfaction. People forget that all the other things in their life don't change, even in the new circumstances, and they find that they're the same person with the same problems.

Stone reports that people with high family income report more intense negative emotions and greater anxiety than people with lower economic status. All this seems to suggest that we need to take a long look at our myth about money so we don't spend our lives working night and day for something that in the end won't satisfy us or make us happy. What Stone and Kahneman are suggesting is that our internal life trumps our external life. The goal is to be personally happy and externally secure, and money is only a part of the solution.

For those who have money, it represents freedom to go and do what they want when they want. Having lots of it takes away money worries. In our society money is power, and for some it's an aphrodisiac. For others money is the measure of success and self-esteem. Many people use money to communicate how successful they are or who they want others to think they are. There are also those who use money to get attention or approval and to make themselves feel they are worthwhile and important.

But how does money play out in our emotions? Do we fear that we cannot be loved or that we won't keep our friends if we don't have money? Are we ashamed about money? Does money enable us to feel more adequate? Does money separate and differentiate us from others? Do we think we are measured by the money yardstick?

Couples who have worked out their issues around money have beaten the odds. In traditional relationships, money can create conflict simply because one person is making the money and the other is at home taking care of the children or not working. There is no paycheck for being a stay-at-home parent or taking care of a household. The one who makes the money often feels more proprietary about how it's being spent and may want to be the one who dispenses it. Among couples who haven't worked through their power dynamic or self-esteem as it relates to money, it can be a source of conflict and bad feeling. Both partners can become resentful if they don't feel appreciated for their contribution to the relationship.

Two very important elements for making agreements about money is for both people to be well-informed as to how much they have to spend, and then to put agreements in place about how they want to spend it.

Agreements About Money Are Made of This

- Developing a plan that includes values, priorities, and available money for spending helps to define personal goals and interests. Special bank accounts for different activities help create spending boundaries, such as a vacation savings account. Home furnishing, remodeling, travel, and recreation can also be included in separate accounts. The key is never to spend money you don't have.

- People often disagree about spending priorities. Sometimes one wants to enjoy life now and the other wants to save for the future. Hammering out a philosophy about spending can eliminate future conflicts. Work out a balance between some money for now and some for later.

- Do you feel that you are a team when it comes to how you spend money? No matter who is making the money or who makes more of it, there needs to be a sense of equality in decisions about how to spend it or there will be resentment. Teamwork is essential and needs to include each person's interests and needs.

- Listing the available cash and limits on spending helps to define effective boundaries. *Golden rules for money*: Treat credit cards like a checkbook and never spend more than you can pay off at the end of the month. Always save ten percent of what you make. Keep three months of operating expenses in a liquid account. But if you aren't able to do this, as Andrew Carnegie once said, "The best way to make money is to not spend it."

- Try not to use money as a means of control, to feel better about yourselves or to soothe your depression. Set aside agreed upon amounts of money and then be willing to renegotiate as the situation requires.

- Importantly, if couples agree on the value of a balanced budget, they will usually fall into an agreeable spending pattern. It's when people use money for emotional gratification that spending can spiral out of control.

Bill and Lucy

Bill and Lucy were college sweethearts. They married shortly after graduation and soon gave birth to a baby girl. Bill became a stockbroker. As he began to make large commissions, he and Lucy bought an old house and hastily began remodeling it. Instead of being just a remodel, it turned out to be a money pit and ate through their finances like a virus. At the same time the stock market took a downturn, and they soon found themselves in financial hot water. They fought bitterly over the money that was hemorrhaging into the seemingly endless remodel. Bill wanted to please Lucy by giving her what she wanted and she wanted the best of everything. When the bills came in, he blew a gasket. Out of sheer desperation they sought therapy. Lucy couldn't understand what was making Bill so angry. After all, she was simply trying to make a beautiful home for him. He was completely at a loss as to why Lucy needed everything to be so top-of-the-line. Taking a look at their past yielded the reason for Lucy's spending spree and Bill's difficulty with setting boundaries for spending.

Lucy had grown up in the poorest family in an affluent suburb. Her father was ashamed of his inability to earn more money and compared himself unfavorably to his more well-heeled neighbors. He hid his comparative financial inadequacy with ostentatious efforts to display his seeming wealth. He was also arrogant and critical of everyone around him. The family value was that money made for personal worth. The more money one had the better person they were. He wanted Lucy to marry into wealth. Lucy was anxious to please her critical and judgmental father. She dreamed of wealth and social position so she could resolve her father's shame of never being rich enough. Her father concealed the truth about their finances until they finally went bankrupt.

Lucy's poor self-esteem drove her to buy expensive items for the house much like her father's efforts to gain approval. The house became the symbol of her self-worth. She was determined once and for all to show the world that she was upper-class and therefore acceptable.

Bill's family was more affluent than Lucy's but also placed a great deal of importance on having money. They owned a small business but made it seem to the world that it was more than it was. His mother was extremely controlling and pressured her children to go to college and major in business. His father was a poor businessman, so his mother prevailed in convincing Bill to be the family savior. Bill's self-esteem was tied to his mother because his father was emotionally absent. When she was angry with Bill, she would disappear into the business and withdraw from him. His mother's emotional disconnects caused Bill to become insecure and fearful of abandonment. When he met Lucy, he became vulnerable to trying to make her happy as a way to keep her connected to him emotionally. He felt that the only way he could stave off being rejected for not being good enough was to give Lucy everything she wanted. His self-esteem became firmly attached to never saying no to her. Then he would resent her for doing what she wanted. He secretly felt that the only reason she was with him was for the material advantages he gave her.

As the remodeling got more and more out of control, Bill's self-esteem issues blocked him from telling Lucy that they couldn't afford what she was spending on the house. He felt inadequate to fulfill Lucy's needs. He believed that if she knew of their limited financial circumstances she would leave him. So he lied to her about his money troubles while behind the scenes he tried to work out deals to delay payments. Eventually they were hopelessly in debt. Lucy found a pile of unpaid bills and soon creditors began calling the house. Bill's worst fears were realized when Lucy threatened to leave him. She accused him of being a poor provider, weak, and a liar for trying to hide his troubles from her. She was full of contempt for Bill and terrified that someone would find out about their financial troubles.

They entered therapy angry and on the brink of divorce. Slowly, they began to understand the roots of what was causing the problems they were facing. Lucy was overcompensating for her low self-esteem by trying to create the perfect upscale home. Bill was trying to hold onto Lucy by giving her what she wanted, but couldn't keep up with her need for approval. As their deeper motivations became clear, they felt more compassionate toward each other. They devised a plan to pull themselves from the brink of financial ruin. They realized during their struggle to become more financially stable that their family mattered more than anything else. Lucy agreed to a budget, and Bill began a payment plan to reduce their debts. They worked on their relationship to make it more satisfying. They realized that spending money was not an adequate substitute for a life and was not a solution to their sense of personal deprivation. They worked to develop a life together, and their efforts helped to strengthen their emotional connection. They discovered that their headlong drive to show the world how valuable they were was only making them angry and depressed. As they developed a more deeply satisfying relationship, their need to spend decreased.

To illustrate how money can affect families, I refer to the story of the Rothschild and the Levy families during WWII. They held the richest and most powerful banking empires in Europe at the time. Hitler's henchmen abducted members of each family and held them for ransom. The Rothschild family decided to pay the ransom, and the Levy family for whatever reason, did not pay. As a consequence, the Levy family split due to the acrimony that ensued, and their wealth eventually dissipated. The Rothschild name remains synonymous with wealth and power and they are still a prominent banking family in Europe. The lesson here is that family unity matters more than money, and a united family will ultimately be more successful, financially or otherwise.

Knowing What You Want

Couples who beat the odds agree on what kind of relationship they want. Many couple conflicts are based on disagreements about social roles and how much time to spend together or with friends and family. How do we want to be with friends? How much time makes sense to be away from each other? Does one person want to spend more time with family and friends than the other? Is it okay to have opposite-sex friends? Is it okay with our mate if we are friends with former lovers or ex-spouses? Who is going to work and who will stay home, or are both expected to work?

When we consider cultural and gender differences, moral and values, we run into innumerable possible disagreements. Working out those issues one by one will save future conflicts from arising. Some couples feel the same about friends and family and others do not. For example, many men want bonding time with their friends. Women, in general, are more relationship-bound and often want time to socialize as a couple. This leads to tension when their mate wants to spend time alone with friends. If men aren't ready for the constraints of a relationship some trouble will ensue. On the other hand, if women become too pressuring and limiting with their husbands, the men may become resentful. Couples who beat the odds are able to find a happy medium between what each one wants and in the process actively create harmony.

Tradition

There is no preeminent relationship style that works better than any other. Whether we're in a traditional or non-traditional type of relationship, the goal is to agree on what kind of relationship we want. In traditional relationships one person stays at home, often taking care of the family, while the other works. A traditional relationship is usually bound by marriage, and as each person is occupied with quite different activities during the day, there are distinctly dissimilar desires for contact at night. The person coming home from a long day out in the world may not want to talk much, while the person who has been alone all day may want to have social contact the minute their partner walks through the door. The partner who is in the workplace is getting paid, which is a positive affirmation. The stay-at-home parent is doing childcare (which tends to be selfless) housework, and running errands. There is not as much external self-esteem support for stay-at-home parents as there is for the working parent, so they may need more expressions of appreciation.

The stay-at-home parent tends to think more about the relationship because of the many visual and social reminders. The partner who is working tends to think less about the other because of their different setting. When the couple meets at the end of the day, their psychology is different because of their vastly dissimilar experiences. If children are present, then those experiences will be even more varied. A common scenario with children is that the mother is tired and wants a break from childcare, while the husband wants to come home and relax. This differing condition can create clashes. So some type of timeframe needs to be established to readjust to different personal needs. Couples who beat the odds find ways to allow for those differences such as giving the person arriving home some time to decompress from the day, and then taking some time to connect. Men tend to need appreciation for bringing in income and women want an emotional connection. When couples learn to express concern, interest, appreciation and acknowledge each other's efforts to work as a team they are effectively beating the odds.

In the more non-traditional relationship, both partners have had a similar workday and often share corresponding sets of experiences. It's potentially easier to divide chores at home because the situation is more equal. Conflicts occur in relationships where both people work, but one is doing more than the other. When couples become active participants in their relationship, they take the time to sit down and divide the chores. One suggestion is to find out what each person likes to do and work out an acceptable routine for getting things done

My compassion for the complexity of relationships is compounded by knowing what people have endured as they have grown up, only to create the same conditions in their love relationships without realizing it. When I hear how families have turned their backs on their children, and how they have abused, neglected, and hurt them, I can only feel a sense of awe that their offspring will try so valiantly to find love even when they feel so undeserving of it. When we can see how we are expressing our anger, what it means, and how it affects our mate, we eventually may be able to throw off the chains of our past and truly move forward into a loving, accepting, and intimate relationship. Couples who endure have successfully created an environment of respect, concern, empathy, safety and security.

It is the conditional aspect of relationships that inevitably keeps them safe. If we feel like there will be no consequences for bad behavior we will be less likely to reflect on it. If on the other hand, we fully understand that our mate will be gone if we don't treat them properly, it will definitely make us think twice about our actions, especially if we truly want to stay with that person. No one should accept poor treatment because they love someone. If a man knows that his temper and his self-centered behavior will end the relationship, he will try hard to respect those boundaries. Without conditions, there will be those who will cross the line and behave thoughtlessly. To define what we want and need from each other helps to determine the way we want to be loved. If friendship, caring, and respect are the conditions of our acceptance, then positive behavior can create love. When these values are a function of love, then we know what we have to do to preserve it. Maintaining positive behavior is sometimes difficult, but it's the challenge of enduring relationships. Whatever we can't see or understand about our past can doom us to repeat it.

Perseverance

What causes some couples to persevere under difficult circumstances and others to simply quit when the going gets tough? Couples who beat the odds are able to persevere long enough to find solutions to difficulties and conflicts. Our ability to do this is complicated and requires strength of character and commitment. Couples who persevere are committed to working until a solution is reached. Often this is done through carefully orchestrated discussions over a period of time. It's important to persevere all the way to the end of a problem without losing our temper and being critical or contemptuous. Working the problem all the way through to a mutually agreed upon resolution is a way to internalize the solution. In this way we will hopefully not encounter the same problem again. While it's true that personal issues don't go away altogether, our ability to understand and discuss those issues is critical to easing the tension arising from them.

The benefits of going all the way to the end of arguments are that they may go away permanently, or that doing so will at least lead to longer periods of harmony. If we can see conflict as constructive and as a direction or goal, we're on the right track. Couples who actively work on eliminating tension and pain have an excellent chance of enjoying a happy relationship. Relationship stability is created by balancing our work life, our need for intellectual stimulation, our desire for connection, our duty to our health, and our commitment to our relationship as a holistic encounter with the world of each other.

The Road to a Healthy Relationship

Susan Johnson writes in *The Practice of Focused Couple Therapy: Creating Connection* that adult love is "a bond, an emotional tie with an irreplaceable other who provides a secure base from which to confront the world and a safe haven, a source of comfort, care and protection." Creating a loving relationship is indeed complex. Ironically, the trick is to do the work to make it simple. But simplicity is a complex task. Our ability to look both within ourselves and between each other to grasp the true source of our unique relationship tango allows us to learn the language of our emotions, and creates a window to the source of our differences and longings. By understanding the layers of our personality, we're not only building a connection with our inner life but also communicating this knowledge to those we love, which inevitably leads us toward a deeper and more lasting connection.

Lasting Intimacy Is Created From:

- Honesty
- Acceptance
- Trust and trustworthiness
- Kindness
- Caring
- Empathy
- Surrender
- Tenderness
- Understanding
- Compassion
- Emotional generosity
- Humor
- Risking expressing our true feelings.

When people view themselves as lovable and their mate as reliable and positive, the result is a secure attachment style. Realistic expectations foster trust and closeness. When each person in a relationship is capable of expressing needs and longings in a safe environment, then a positive relationship process results.

Thomas H. Maugh II, a medical writer for the *Los Angeles Times*, discusses another key element that creates loss and dissolution. He writes, "Marriages that did work well all had one thing in common; the husband was willing to listen to the wife." He found that only those newlywed men who were "accepting influence" from their wives were ending up in happy, stable marriages. John Gottman, in *The Seven Principles of a Happy Marriage*, describes the critical piece to marriage happiness in this way: "The autocrats, who failed to listen to their wives' complaints, greeting them with stonewalling, contempt, and belligerence, were doomed from the beginning." He goes on to say that most women do listen to their husbands. He did not let women completely off the hook though. "Women who couched their complaints in a gentle even humorous approach to the husband were more likely to have happy marriages than those who were more belligerent."

The principles that seem to hold true about love-making are: *If we are self-critical, we will be critical with others. If we are depressed, our relationship will be depressed. If we feel insecure, we will have an insecure relationship.* There is no way around how internal pain affects our relations with others. Self-knowledge is relationship power. Self-knowledge accesses relationships, and relationships access self-knowledge. An emotional bond with another person strengthens our ability to heal personal wounds, to restore our precious sense of connection, and to create a safe place to love and be loved.

We all have basic rights in relationships. Patricia Evans lists the essential relationship rights in her book, *The Verbally Abusive Relationship.*

We Have the Right:

- To emotional support.
- To be heard by the other and be responded to with courtesy.
- To have our own point of view, even if it differs from our partner's.
- To have our feelings and experiences acknowledged as real.
- To live free from accusation and blame.
- To live free from criticism and judgment.
- To live free from emotional and physical threat.
- To live free from angry outbursts and rage.

I include these rights here to underscore the idea that these are basic rights that all of us should expect to give and get in a healthy relationship. Many people who were raised in households that did not respect these basic rights do not even know they deserve better treatment.

Couples who beat the odds take an easy or humorous approach to life's difficulties. They know the power of the positive and how to eliminate the negative in creating loving feelings. These couples are able to recognize and take responsibility for their actions and take an active approach to problem solving. Successful couples accept themselves, and are able to be respectful no matter how angry they may feel. What makes relationships so valuable is that *we have to be better people to make them work and to be in them.*

11

And They Lived Happily Ever After....

We don't see things as they are. We see things as we are.

Anaïs Nin

In this final chapter I would like to revisit some of the main concepts that I have found to be most helpful, so that couples can do some work with them on their own. The point of this book is to make each of us think about what's important in our love relationships and how we can go about making the changes that will further our own personal and relationship evolution.

One by-product of self-knowledge is that we're better able to express our feelings, needs, and wants. When couples go off the rails, it's often because they feel they must ramp up the volume and intensity to get through to each other. The most common issue for dysfunctional interaction is the failure to acknowledge what our partner is telling us. Acknowledging each other's thoughts and feelings does not necessarily mean we must agree. The fact that we feel heard and understood is often enough to end the conflict. When couples cycle around and around in angry exchanges, they are defending instead of acknowledging. Once couples can simply acknowledge what's being said, they're actively moving toward resolution.

How Our Moods Affect What We See

Our moods shape our perceptions and our responses to each other. If we pay attention to them and learn to recognize how our partner is responding to us, we will be able to determine exactly how our moods are affecting our perspective. When a present experience mirrors our past, it stimulates what Christopher Bollas terms an "emotional memory." In his book *The Shadow of the Object,* Bollas describes moods as emotional memories that represent a present stimulus to one of our early experiences. Our ability to understand what our moods are telling us about our history and ultimately ourselves is critical to working through them. Distinguishing what's triggering our moods provides precious insight into what we're afraid of so we can work through it with our partner. Bringing old fears out of the darkness of our unknown helps us to see that they're simply old memories and not present reality. Bollas also talks about what he describes as an "unthought known." What he means by this is that we *know* something is bothering us or that we feel less than others, but we don't really *think* about it. He believes that bringing those "unthought knowns" into consciousness allows us to process them and eventually change the way we believe ourselves to be.

J. H. Van Den Berg recounts a story that illustrates this point. He writes in *A Different Existence* about how our feelings color and shape our sense of reality. He tells the story of a young man waiting in a mountain cabin for his lover to arrive. The room is aglow with light from the fireplace, and bright with the anticipation of meeting his true love in their hilltop hideaway. Beside him sits a bottle of wine. The wine appears beautiful to him through his desire and glistens in the firelight, as the room takes on the essence of this desire. The phone rings and he learns that his lover is not coming and will never come. He sinks into a depression. Suddenly, the fire appears menacing, and the once glowing room seems gloomy and foreboding. The wine that only moments before appeared to be so divine now looks repulsive to him. Clearly it was not the room but his feelings that changed. This story illustrates one of the tenets of this book: that our inner life affects the way we perceive reality and is based on our perspective. Jean Paul Sartre said that "reality is perspectival." It is our perspective that changes with the ebb and flow of emotion and then influences our sense of reality. If our inner experience is depressed, fearful, insecure, and hateful, these struggles will taint our perception and will restrict or affect action and reactions to ourselves and others.

The cornerstone of all interactions with others is our ability to recognize what we're experiencing within, and then to apply that knowledge and perspective to our current interaction. No matter how we begin a relationship, our ability to sustain it lovingly over time is an active process that should be resolution-oriented and responsive to the other person. We fall in love naturally, but to preserve it requires that we process our thoughts and feelings in a positive way. People usually begin relationships with a high degree of sexuality, but it cannot remain vital if conflicts and resentments aren't resolved. To stay together, couples need to work together to develop mutually satisfying activities, create connections, craft shared values, develop a friendship, and commit to an active problem-solving process. Working out agreements along with efforts to repair breaks in our emotional bond helps to create a lasting love.

The most common problem for couples is their inability to resolve basic conflicts. Using some very simple guidelines, couples can easily resolve many everyday quarrels. When in a conflict ask yourself the following questions:

Reparation Made Easy

- What is my responsibility in the current conflict?
- What are my partner's feelings and thoughts about the problem?
- Have I acknowledged what my partner is trying to tell me?
- Am I or is my partner in a bad mood, tired, or irritated about something else?
- What feelings, needs, and wants are being expressed?
- What could both of us do to make it better?
- What could we do differently next time?

The unswerving truth that so many of us are unwilling to consider is that in many ways we control how people feel about us. This does not mean we must be phony. On the contrary, if we express how we truly and deeply feel with empathy, compassion and kindness we are more likely to create a positive result. Most couple discord occurs because we are too afraid to express our truth. Instead, we become defensive or critical. But if we are willing to risk being truthful about our feelings, are able to set boundaries if necessary, are thoughtful, caring, and considerate in the way we express our truth, we are much more likely to resolve problems. Frequently I observe couples being negative with each other when at the bottom of it they just want to know that the other one cares about them. They will get angry, blame, and be righteous about all kinds of things rather than risk their feelings being exposed. It's difficult for couples to peel back the layers and see that deep in their hearts they are just crying out for love.

When couples complain they are usually objecting to some kind of unfair or unkind treatment. But what are almost always lying beneath negative interactions are longings to be cared about, accepted and loved. When couples become dysfunctional, it's almost always because they don't know enough about who they are and how their personal issues are affecting their responses to their mate.

When issues cycle around, it's usually because neither person will admit to their part in the problem and instead feel entitled to be critical, angry and blaming. When the victim becomes the aggressor, no resolution is possible. It becomes an endless tit-for-tat. More often then not, when I'm in treatment with a dysfunctional couple, it's because they're so focused on what the other one did wrong that they are unable or unwilling to see and/or admit what they are doing to create their fifty percent of the problem. If each person could own up to their part and acknowledge the feelings of their partner, most conflicts would promptly disappear. It's also not unusual to find that people have no idea what lies deeply within them because their shame is hidden even from themselves. Once the deeper process is understood, the therapy can work to heal the wound and this will positively affect their relationship: "Oh, I'm sorry that I hurt your feelings; I was hurt because I felt rejected and alone. I love you, I miss you and I need you." When this kind of dialogue is expressed, it creates a connection.

To resolve conflicts we need to join with our mate in the problem-solving process. *When we become a true partner, we recognize the need to put the welfare of the relationship before our particular point of view.* Risking exposing our hurt and vulnerability is an important step on the road to loving more deeply. Our ability to apologize to our partner for causing any pain is essential to healing the inevitable broken connections. What's important is not that we will break connections but that we know how to repair them. Creating a loving atmosphere requires attention. From attentiveness we make connections. This process can be as simple as waiting for our partner when we leave a restaurant, putting our arm around them when we're walking, or simply checking in at the end of the day.

If we believe that bonds will never break we are in for a disappointment. Loving kindness moves us toward each other, just as needing to be right and blaming moves us away. We do not have to find compassion first—we can find it along the way—but the important point is to look for it. Reparation is integral to intimacy. Suppose we have acted insensitively toward our mate, and they are hurt. Expressing concern and regret creates closeness. Being critical and sarcastic will push them away.

Does Short Term Therapy Help?

Currently we are experiencing a myriad of media-generated therapies offering quick and easy solutions to a whole host of psychological problems ranging from marital conflicts to self-esteem issues. It's not that what they're saying isn't helpful, but the problem is that it's often only a piece of the truth and not the whole truth. And those who think it is may be disappointed. For instance, self-esteem issues can be very complex. They often take some time to unravel. From many years of doing therapy I have come to a place where I respect the often vexing complexities of human experience. Finding lasting solutions often demands that we look into the deeper complexity. This does not mean that psychotherapy must always be complex and long-term. But not all solutions are simple. For example, building trust with a person who has never trusted anyone may take some time. To respect each person's uniqueness requires an equally unique approach. To use therapy as if it were a cookie-cutter process is fundamentally disrespectful to the individual. Many people gain tremendous insight and better feelings from some of the more short term therapies. But there are also people who go into these processes expecting a quick cure and are terribly overwrought when they subsequently revert to their original behavior. Therapists need to make people aware that their issues are important and help them to find solutions to their difficulties in a variety of modalities.

Encouraging people to stay to the finish line is difficult when all they hear in pop culture are easy fixes. If I have learned anything, it's that people are doing the best they can. So no matter how self-destructive their behavior seems, to ask them to remove what they may feel is a life-sustaining defense or some other process that makes them feel good about themselves is not what may help them. It's often better to build more strength first and then slowly remove the negative behavior. In this way we can be inclusive and not exclusive.

On Being an Objective Observer

The ability to observe ourselves from an objective point of view is an important part of relationship success. This means that we are seeing things as they actually are instead of through our often distorted subjectivity. Building objectivity is done best when both people reflect together and create a sense of who they are within and between each other. Without this objectivity we are doomed to a subjective distortion that can pump out negativity into the system of our relationship. As children, we needed to keep an emotional connection with our parents to feel safe. Children have not developmentally acquired the ability to be objective, so they always believe that they're responsible for the pain they feel. As adults, we want to build an objective sense of the world and ourselves, which requires another person to reflect back to us what they see. We need to trust what they see as truth and then process it as a part of who we are.

To be subjective as a child is essential for emotional survival. To be subjective as an adult can create conflict. For example: A man is waiting for his wife to get ready, and she is once again running late. He becomes impatient and angrily protests, "Can't you ever be on time?" She snaps back at him, "I'm going as fast as I can." He counters with, "It always has to be on your timetable; it's never about what I need." He could have predicted her response, yet he can't let it go. He berates her, and the argument becomes an exchange of furious and insulting defensive remarks. This creates a deadlock of dark emotion and they become distant and silent. He feels that he is entirely justified because after all, it was she who was once again late. Had he understood why he was so angry with her lateness, his initial response could have been short-circuited. Perhaps as a child he had often waited for his mother to pick him up from school when it rained, and she either would come late or would forget altogether. He might have a serious set of sad and angry feelings about lateness. If he had known and understood this about himself it could have helped him to find better solutions to his wife's lateness. But if he objectively understands that his wife is not abandoning him as his mother did and is just a late person, then he will be less inclined to be so angry when she's late. Then he can decide to talk to her about their mutual issue at a more conducive time, and they can come to some agreement about possible solutions. He may be able to busy himself with some worthwhile activity while he waits, and she can try to plan better so that when she's ready they can leave knowing that his prodding won't hurry her up or make the evening go more smoothly. Building an objective view helps us to know where the pain is coming from so that the problems associated with that pain can be avoided.

There are many issues that come up for couples again and again. The point is determining which issues we can change and which will remain as stable internal systems. We also need to understand which issues put our relationship at risk so we can do something about them before it's too late.

Is Your Relationship at Risk?

- Are you angry with your mate more than twice a week?
- Do you find yourself unable to resolve arguments?
- Do you feel that your partner does not listen?
- Do you find yourself always needing to be right?
- Do you frequently argue over what each of you said?

- Do you defend yourself most of the time during arguments?
- Do you frequently blame your mate for your anger?
- Do you withdraw from your partner?
- Do you secretly criticize your mate?
- Do you become violent when you're angry?
- Do arguments easily escalate into rage?
- Do you have frequent depressions?
- Do you have expectations that exceed your partner's ability?
- Is it hard for you to compliment your mate?
- Do you take sides against your mate in conflicts with others?
- Are there substance abuse problems?
- Do arguments often end with silence?
- Are you having an affair?
- Do you lack sexual desire for your partner?
- Do you feel contempt for your partner?
- Have you lost respect for your partner?
- Are you unhappy with your mate more than 50% of the time?

If you answered yes to some of these questions, your relationship may be at risk.

As we choose a life partner, there are certain traits and conditions that we must look for before we make the most important decision of our lives. These life choices are not always considered so objectively. We often go with sexual attraction and initial intense feelings. There are important guidelines that we must consider if we are to be successful in a relationship over time.

Some Basic Concepts to Consider When Choosing a Life Partner:

- What is their history, including their relationship with their parents?

- Do they have good relationships with both parents?
- Did they have a satisfying youth?
- Were they abused or neglected?
- Are there drug or alcohol issues?
- Does their self-esteem depend on approval from others?
- Do you share similar values, moral, religious, and spiritual beliefs?
- Do you share the same life goals?
- Do you feel comfortable with each other?
- Do you feel respected and accepted?
- Is there a sense of equality?
- Are you sexually compatible?
- Can you be tender toward each other?
- Is he/she generous?
- Do you agree on what kind of relationship you want to have?
- Can the two of you find the humor in situations?
- Are they affectionate in a similar way that you are?
- Do they have a good sense of humor?
- Are they able to relax?
- Do they have a moral code that agrees with yours?
- Is he/she your friend?
- Do you feel safe and secure?
- Has your partner done any personal work (psychotherapy) or significant self-reflection?
- Is he/she a good listener?
- Are there unresolved anger issues?
- Are they good at resolving conflicts?
- Do you have similar ideas about family and children?
- How do you each feel about in-laws and/or children from a former marriage?

If we think our parents are not as significant to us as adults as when we were children, let me tell you a story about my father. About ten years ago when my father lay dying, we were alone at his bedside. He looked at me with great sincerity and for the first time told me that he was proud of me and that he loved me. He wanted to make it right between us. In the end, all that mattered to him was his family. He wanted to make sure I knew how much he loved me. In that moment all the pain that was between us fell away, and I was left with an affectionate and loving feeling toward him. Here I was a grown man how my father felt about me still affected me. Our parents remain important figures in our lives and can help us understand our current relationships. Many people never get the opportunity to make amends with their parents living or dying. It's an emotionally healthy act to resolve past conflicts with our parents and family if we can.

The power of love comes back to me in the work I do, through all my own explorations and within my marriage and family. When it's all said and done, it appears that our ability to express and accept love is what makes life worth living. It is love after all that spins the ordinary into the extraordinary.

Love-making means creation. It's an extension of our heart's desire and how we express it to one another. What I often observe is that people will endure great hardships for love, *once they know what it is.* Love is the luminosity that lifts us from the drudgery of our everyday lives. To keep the flame of passion burning, couples need to reach beyond what feels safe, to risk rejection, in order to love more deeply. If we can persevere in our striving to love each other, we will more often than not be rewarded for our efforts. Love-making is the ability to liberate the energy of love so it can flow freely between us. The work is to remove what blocks our ability to love and to encourage us to speak our truth and risk opening our heart. A wise colleague of mine once said that there is no way to have a completely safe life and still live it.

The work of love is to create love. The goal is to make conflict resolution into intimacy creation. When we can depend on each other for understanding, caring, patience, perseverance, and tenderness we make our relationship safe and secure. An apt metaphor for relationships is to liken them to the earth, with love being the atmosphere. When it's autumn we prepare for impending challenges by making time for each other. So when winter does come, we can keep out the cold and make a warm fire. When it's spring, we celebrate. In the heat of summer, we seek the cool of a shade tree. We know when our relationship is loving and the atmosphere feels sweet. The goal is to keep our thoughts and feelings positive so we're living where the relationship temperature feels just right. When the climate between each other is warm and there is a soft breeze blowing in off the ocean of positive feelings our lives feel uplifted. Knowing what to do when the weather changes can help create and maintain a loving atmosphere.

In the years of working with families, I am continually amazed at the capacity of people to both withstand and repair their broken connections. The challenge for couples is to learn how to mend breaks in their emotional bond and to develop new methods for resolving relationship problems. If we can decipher the difference between what we *think* we see and what is so hard to see, and if we listen for the truth when everything in us is screaming, "It's them," we are on our way to finding the secret that unlocks the door to the love we want.

A patient once said to me that relationships are relentless. They are that and more. Who we are is before us, under us, between us and between the lines. The truth is if we want to love deeply we cannot hide either from ourselves or from the ones we love. Love offers the ultimate challenge: not just accepting our own obvious imperfections, but also loving our partner not in spite of their flaws, but *because* of them. To reach into our soul and find the meaning of our current crisis is what love-making requires. Our willingness to be open, to continue to persevere and be lifted up by the exquisite radiance of love continues to answer the question, "Why love?"

Love must be as much a light as it is a flame.
Henry David Thoreau

Epilogue

What it takes....

If you can place love before anger
and reach into your darkness to hold on

If you can lead with heart instead of hurt
and know the difference between the two

If you can make kindness more important than rightness
and listen with your mind wide open

If you can keep your head on straight when it's screaming for revenge and somehow find compassion's truth

If you can make gentleness and humor your way of saying hard
things and not use honesty as a weapon of choice

If you can give what you need the most
and not fall victim to being the victim

If you can make the needs of others more important than your own
yet not be afraid to ask for what you want

If you can accept that conflict is a given and trust is earned
and not expect others to reach your unreachable ideals

If you know that love is made from being a loving person
and can weave it into each day in some way

If you can be what is best about you
and know the difference between you and me

If you can keep your fears in balance
when all you want to do is run for cover

If you can let your love be the light
that leads your way back home

If you can be respectful with your words
and courageous with your heart

Then you will know what it means to love.

References

Ackerman, Diane, *The Natural History of Love* (Vintage Press, 1995)

Ainsworth, Mary, *Basic Books* (1990)

Ainsworth, Mary D. Salter, *Infancy in Uganda; infant care and growth of love.*

Baltimore, *Johns Hopkins Press* (1967)

Anand, Margot, *The Art of Sexual Ecstasy: The Path of Sacred Sexuality for Western Lovers* (Jeremy P. Tarcher, 1989)

Ardry, J. Richard, *The Social Context of Marriage* (J. B. Lippincott, 1966)

Bach, George R., *Pairing* (Mass Market Paperback, Avon Books, 1973

Barnes, Hazel E., *Humanistic Existentialism: The Literature of Possibility* (University of Nebraska Press, 1959)

Barry, M. J., *Depression, Shame, Loneliness and the Psychiatrist's Position* (American Journal of Psychiatry, 1962, p.16)

Bollas, Christopher, *The Shadow of The Object: Psychoanalysis of the Unthought Unknown* (Columbia University Press, 1989)

Bowlby, John, *Attachment: Attachment and Loss* (vol. 1) (Basic Books, 1969)

Buss, David M., *Evolutionary Psychology.* (Allyn and Bacon 1st Edition, 1998)

Cloke, Kenneth, *Crossroads of Conflict: A Journey into the Heart of Dispute Resolution* (Janis Publications, 2006)

Craske, Michelle, *Mastery of Your Anxiety and Panic* (Oxford University Press, 2006)

De Beauvoir, Simone, *Second Sex* (Knopf Publishing Group, 1990)

De Bernie_res, Louis, *Corelli's Mandolin* (Vintage Books, 1995)

Estes, Clarissa Pincola, *Verbal Abuse. Survivors Speak Out: On Relationship and Recovery. Edition 1.* (Abrams Media. 2003)

Evans, Patricia, *The Verbally Abusive Relationship* (Adams Media, 2 Exp Sub Edition, 2003)

Gilligan, Carol, *In a Different Voice* (Harvard University Press, 1993)

Goffman, Erving, *The Presentation of Self in Everyday Life* Edition 1. (Anchor Press, 1959)

Gottman, John & Silver, Nan, *The Seven Principles of Making a Marriage Work; A Practical Guide from the Country's Foremost Relationship Expert* (Crown Publishers, 1999)

Grosskurth, Phyllis, *Melanie Klein; Her World and Her Work* (Aronson, 1995)

Hite, Shere, *The Hite Report* (Dell, 1987)

Husten, Ted & Coughlin, John & Houtz, Renate & Smith, Shanna & George, Laura. *The Connubial Crucible: Newlywed Years as Predictors of Marital Delight, Distress and Divorce.* Journal of Personality and Social Psychology, 2001. Vol. 80, pp.237-252.

Johnson, Susan, *The Practice of Emotionally Focused Couple Therapy: Creating Connection* (Brunner/Routledge, 2004)

Jong, Erica, *Fear of Flying* (Henry Holt & Company, 1973)

Karen, Robert, *Becoming Attached: Psychology's Effort to Understand the Power of First Relationships and How They Impact Our Capacity to Love* (Oxford University Press, 1998)

Kaufman, Gershon, *The Meaning of Shame: Towards a Self-Affirming Identity* (Journal of Counseling Psychology, 1974)

Kaufman, Gershon, *Coming Out of Shame* (Doubleday; 1st Edition, 1995)

Kegan, Robert, *In Over Our Heads: The Mental Demands of Modern Life* (Harvard University Press, 1996)

Kohlberg, Lawrence, *The Philosophy of Moral Development, Moral Stages and the Idea of Justice* (Harper Row, 1st Edition, 1981)

Klein, Melanie, *Love, Hate and Reparation* (W.W. Norton & Company, 1964)

Kiersey, David, *Please Understand Me* (Prometheus Nemesis Book Company, 1984)

Kundera, Milan, *The Unbearable Lightness of Being* (Harper Collins, 2002)

Levi-Strauss, Claude, *Tristes Tropiques* (Criterion Books, 1961)

Malone, Thomas Patrick, *The Art of Intimacy* (Fireside Press. 1988)

Masters, William & Johnson, Virginia, *Masters and Johnson on Sex and Human Loving* (Little, Brown & Company, 1988)

Mead, Margaret, *Sexual Temperament in Three Primitive Societies* (Harper Collins, 1935)

Miller, Alice, *The Drama of The Gifted Child* (Basic Books, 3 Rev Upd Edition, 1996)

Mitchell, Stephen, *The Enlightened Heart* (Harper Perennial, 1993)

Ofman, William V. *Affirmation & Reality* (Western Psychological Services, 1976)

Perel, Esther, *Mating in Captivity: Reconciling the Erotic and the Domestic* (Harper Paperbacks, 2007)

Siegel, Allen M., *Heinz Kohut and the Psychology of Self* Edition 1. (Routledge Press, 1996)

Solomon, Marion, *Lean On Me: The Power of Positive Dependency in Intimate Relationships* (Simon and Schuster, 1994)

Sullivan, Harry Stack, *Erogenous Maturation* (Psychoanalytic Review, Vol. 12, p.30, 1926)

J.H. Van Den Berg, *A Different Existence: Principles of Phenomenological Psychopathology* (Duquesne University Press, 1972)

Wile, Daniel B., *Couples Therapy: A Nontraditional Approach* (John Wiley & Sons, 1981)

Wurmser, Leon, *The Mask of Shame* (Jason Aronson, 1997)

Yudofsky, Stuart C., *Fatal Flaws: Navigating Destructive Relationships with People with Disorders of Personality and Character* (American Psychiatric Publishing, 2005)

About The Author

Dr. Bill Cloke, a psychotherapist in private practice for over 20 years, specializes in working with families, couples, and children. Married for 18 years, and a proud parent and grandparent, Bill has always been intrigued with how the family setting influences behavior. Bill began his career teaching in the Santa Monica Unified School District and now works with individuals and couples from a cross-section of cultures throughout Los Angeles.

"If I can help a family stay together, it is especially good for the children. That's what makes my work so fulfilling," says Dr. Cloke.

Bill's media appearances include being a radio guest psychologist on The Rachel Donahue Show in Santa Barbara, California; an online psychologist for The Parent Club; and a guest psychologist on Joi De Vivre Cable Television. His published articles have been featured in Los Angeles Family Magazine and in Healthy Attitudes.

Dr. Cloke received his B.A. from California State University at Northridge in Anthropology, and was awarded a National Teacher Corps Fellowship, a Life Teaching Credential and an M.S.Ed from the University of Southern California. He holds a Ph.D. in Psychology from California Graduate Institute.

A popular lecturer at UCLA and the Los Angeles Unified School District, he can be reached through his website at www.billcloke.com